Munchies, Dips, Spreads, *and* Breads

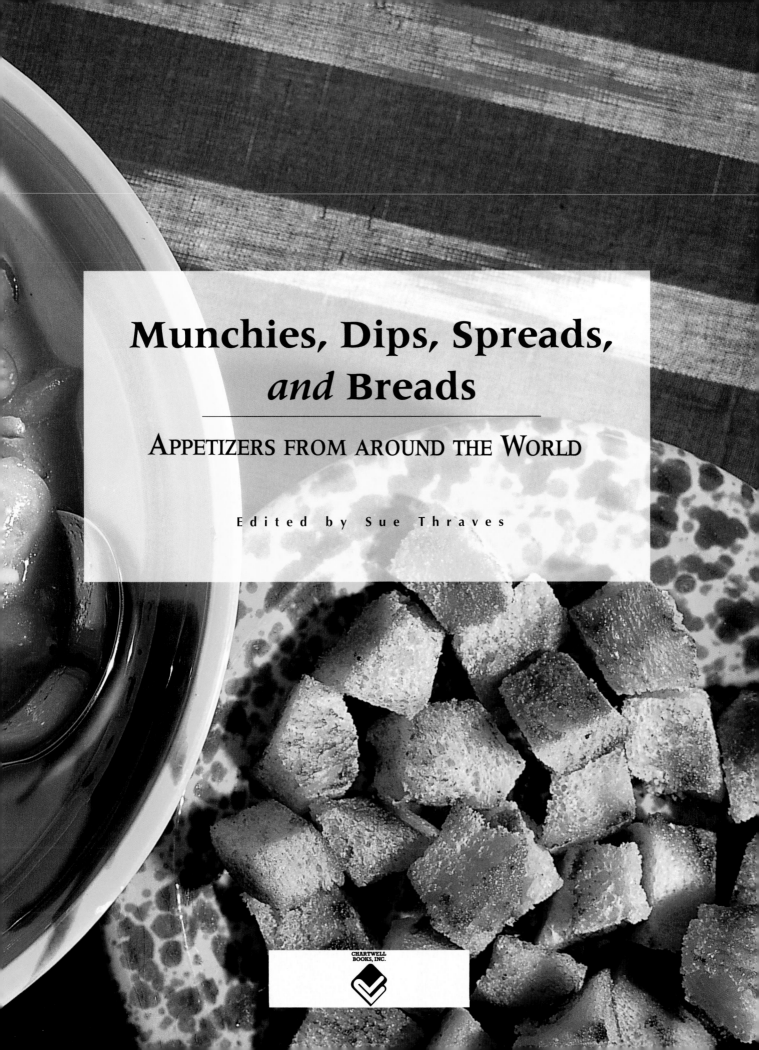

Munchies, Dips, Spreads, *and* Breads

APPETIZERS FROM AROUND THE WORLD

Edited by Sue Thraves

CHARTWELL
BOOKS, INC.

A QUINTET BOOK
Published by Chartwell Books
A Division of Book Sales, Inc.
PO Box 7100
Edison, New Jersey 08818-7100

This edition produced for sale in the U.S.A., its territories
and dependencies only.

ISBN 0-7858-0444-7

This book was designed and produced by
Quintet Publishing Limited
6 Blundell Street
London N7 9BH

Creative Director: Richard Dewing
Designer: Mark Roberts @ Design Revolution
Project Editor: Anna Briffa
Editor: Sue Thraves

Typeset in Great Britain by
Central Southern Typesetters, Eastbourne
Manufactured in Singapore by Bright Arts Pte Ltd
Printed in Singapore by Star Standard Industries (Pte) Ltd

The material in this publication previously appeared in:
*Cajun Cooking, Caribbean Cooking, Chinese Vegetarian
Cooking, Classic Chinese and Oriental Cooking, Creole
Cooking, The Fresh Pasta Cookbook, The Great Garlic
Cookbook, The Hot and Spicy Cookbook, Indian Low-Fat
Cooking, Indian Vegetarian Cooking, Modern and
Traditional Irish Cooking, Italian Trattoria Cooking,
Lebanese Cooking, Mexican Cooking, Meze Cooking,
New Jewish Cooking, Nuevo Cubano Cooking, Recipes
from a Polish Kitchen, Russian Regional Recipes, Salsa
Cooking, Southern Cooking, Spanish Cooking, Stir Fry
Cooking, Tapas, Thai Cooking, Vegetarian Pasta Cooking,
Vietnamese Cooking.*

C O N T E N T S

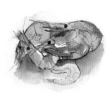

Appetizers from around the World

INTRODUCTION

APPETIZERS FROM AROUND THE WORLD IS A FABULOUS COLLECTION OF DELICIOUS LUNCHES, DIPS,

SPREADS, COLD BITES, HOT BITES, SOUPS, SALADS AND HOMEMADE BREADS TO SERVE AT COCKTAIL PARTIES,

FORMAL AND INFORMAL DINNER PARTIES, OR LARGE BUFFETS. OVER 200 RECIPES HAVE BEEN SELECTED FROM OVER

TWENTY CUISINES, FROM THE AMERICAS, TO EUROPE, TO THE FAR EAST. THE SEASONINGS AND FLAVORINGS

RANGE FROM SUBTLE TO PIQUANT AND SWEET TO SAVORY. YOU WILL FIND A VARIETY OF VEGETARIAN DISHES FOR

NON-MEAT EATERS, AND FOR THE CALORIE-CONSCIOUS, A SELECTION OF LOW-FAT RECIPES. YOU WILL GAIN

MYRIAD IDEAS FOR A HOST OF MEAL OCCASIONS AND EVEN THOUGH THE COOKING INSTRUCTIONS ARE

EASY TO FOLLOW, THE RESULTS ARE GUARANTEED TO PLEASE.

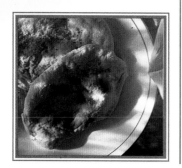

Regional variations

A quick word about some of the regional cuisines in the book. In Italian cookery, antipasti are appetizers served as the first course of a meal. You will find a collection of traditional antipasti recipes in this book. Antipasti may be as simple as oven-crispy bread with tomato and fresh basil, or a combination of some fifteen or more tempting morsels. There are many fish and seafood dishes in this book which are particularly popular in Spanish, Greek and Italian cuisine. Bite-sized pieces are crumbled or lightly buttered, fried and served hot with wedges of lemon. Mexican, Cuban and Caribbean dishes are traditionally spicy, but can be as hot or mild as you like. These cuisines are an amalgam of many influences, fused together and, over a period of time have evolved into more distinct, recognizable styles. Indian, Chinese and Thai cuisines all have highly distinctive but delicious flavors. With these cuisines especially, ordinary vegetables are transformed when combined with wonderful spices and delicious sauces. In Russia, the tradition of serving "Zakuski," a table of small bites or appetizers is a popular feature. You will find an abundance of dishes taken from this continent in the book. Lebanese cuisine is based on traditional Arab cookery which has been influenced by more cosmopolitan flavorings from Europe.

Planning a buffet

If you are planning a buffet meal for twelve people, use the following guidelines: one meat dish, one fish or savory dish, a potato, rice or pasta salad, two other salad dishes, one or two of the bread recipes from the final chapter, and a selection of fresh fruit and cheeses. Do not forget to include a variety of drinks. Beer is perfect with dips, hot nuts and nibbles from Chapter One, and homemade punch is always a good way to break the ice at the start of any party. Do not forget to include a selection of non-alcoholic beverages for guests who are driving and for children. An important point to bear in mind when planning a buffet or a meal with set courses, is to choose dishes with a harmonious balance of colors, flavors, form and texture. The beauty of this book is that the recipes are not too complicated and, with the exception of a few,

the ingredients are not too difficult to find. There are no fancy garnishes or decorations. Often a sprinkling of fresh herbs is all that is needed to transform even the simplest of dishes.

Obtaining your ingredients

Don't be daunted by those dishes that are unfamiliar to you – try them or you'll never know what you've been missing. Spices are invaluable for adding that special blend of heat, fragrance and pungency to a whole range of dishes. Bear in mind however, that some are stronger than

Fish, meat and poultry

Always choose the freshest, best quality fish, meat and poultry you can afford. When buying fish look for firm, even-textured flesh, bright red gills and a clean smell. The flavor of poultry is dependent upon its age. Choose young birds with tender flesh – once cooked the meat will taste mild in flavor. Red meats such as beef and lamb vary in color and texture. Quality beef should have little or no gristle, be plum-red in color and slightly moist. Lamb and pork should be pale pink, again with little fat or gristle. When preparing meat and poultry, take care to trim away any visible fat before cooking. Try to eat red meat in moderation to reduce your consumption of fat as much as possible.

Vegetable, cheese and pasta

Ideally, vegetables should be crisp and firm. Avoid small vegetables – which are probably immature and therefore lacking in flavor. Be as fussy when choosing cheese and avoid anything that looks too dry, hard, soft and, especially if pre-packed, sweaty. In this book you will find many recipes that require pasta. You can use bought pasta or make your own. Homemade really is much nicer, and if you have a pasta machine, it will pay dividends. Oriental noodles and pasta doughs are available from specialist supermarkets.

others. When experimenting with spices, it is wise to start with small amounts – you can always add more depending upon your heat tolerance at a later stage. If you do experience difficulties in obtaining certain ingredients, try to locate a specialist supermarket in your area, or you can order spices from certain companies by mail order. They usually have their own catalog which is free of charge.

Preparation and presentation

Planning ahead is very important whether preparing a formal set course meal or simple canapés for a drinks party. If you are preparing finger food, you will find numerous recipes for appropriate dishes in Chapters One, Two and Three. Always make sure you provide napkins for your guests. Presentation of the food is extremely important, and if you are planning a buffet, a little forethought will be worthwhile. For example, to avoid a confusion of people around the food table, place the drinks, flatware, and

crockery away from the food itself on a separate table. It's also a good idea to prepare food ahead of time so that it can be refrigerated or frozen, then simply defrosted or reheated. The breads, pastry-based recipes such as quiches, and many of the soups are particularly suitable for this.

Some of the simplest appetizers to prepare are dips (see Chapter One). A selection of crisp, young vegetables make an attractive accompaniment. Allow 4–6 ounces of vegetables per person, and choose at least three different varieties. Suitable crudités include carrots, zucchini, celery, and cucumber, each cut into narrow fingers.

Variety is said to be the spice of life, but take care not to overwhelm your guests with an enormous appetizer followed by a huge main course. If you are planning to set a course menu, it is best to include a simple appetizer and a more elaborate main course or vice versa.

You will find *Appetizers from around the World* a constant source of inspiration from the host of traditional favorite recipes to the more exotic surprises with variations on a theme. Remember that first impressions are often the last, and a carefully chosen appetizer or selection of dishes for a buffet will play a crucial role in any successful meal, whatever the occasion.

CHAPTER ONE

Munchies, Dips and Spreads

~

Garlic Buttered Nuts – FRANCE

INGREDIENTS

2 CUPS SHELLED ALMONDS, CASHEWS
   OR PEANUTS, OR A MIXTURE

2 TABLESPOONS BUTTER

1 TABLESPOON OIL

2–3 GARLIC CLOVES, CRUSHED

PINCH OF ROCK SALT

serves 4

METHOD

Loosen and remove the almond skins by pouring boiling water over them and refreshing in cold water. Rub the brown skins off the peanuts. Melt the butter and oil with the garlic in a heavy skillet and toss the nuts in it over a medium heat for 3 to 5 minutes, or until they are crisp and golden. Drain on paper towels, and sprinkle with rock salt. Serve warm.

Spiced Almonds – LEBANON

INGREDIENTS

3 TABLESPOONS SUNFLOWER OIL

2½ CUPS WHOLE BLANCHED ALMONDS

¾ CUP LIGHT BROWN SUGAR

½ TEASPOON GROUND CUMIN

1 TEASPOON DRIED CHILI POWDER

PINCH OF SALT

serves 4

Nuts play a large part in the Levantine diet, and appear as appetizers, in main courses and in desserts. Both spicy and sweet nuts appear as *meze* or snacks; these almonds are a spicy version.

METHOD

Heat the oil in a skillet over a medium to high heat until it is hot. Add the almonds, stirring, together with three-quarters of the sugar. Toss the nuts in the sugar to coat thoroughly, and sauté until the nuts are caramelized. Transfer the nuts to a bowl and toss with the cumin, chili powder and salt to taste. Spread the nuts out on a baking sheet to dry and, while still warm, sprinkle them with the remaining sugar to taste. Serve warm or at room temperature. The nuts will keep for two weeks if they are stored in an airtight container.

Deviled Nuts – INDIA

METHOD

Pour boiling water over the almonds, refresh in cold water, and slip off the skins. Toast the peanuts for 2 minutes, and rub off the skins in a dish towel. Heat the oil and butter in a heavy skillet, and fry the garlic for a few seconds. Add the nuts, reduce the heat to medium, and toss the nuts until crisp and golden, 4 to 6 minutes. Drain on paper towels, and toss in rock salt and cayenne pepper. Serve warm.

Variation For Bombay Beans, substitute canned garbanzo beans for the nuts. Wash and drain them well, and pat dry.

INGREDIENTS

2 CUPS SHELLED ALMONDS, CASHEWS
  OR PEANUTS OR A MIXTURE
1 TABLESPOON OIL
1 TABLESPOON BUTTER
1 GARLIC CLOVE, CRUSHED
PINCH OF ROCK SALT
PINCH OF CAYENNE PEPPER

serves 4

Spiced Nut Mix – EGYPT

This is a traditional Egyptian dish which is eaten scooped up with pocket bread.

METHOD

Preheat the oven to 350°F. Roast the hazelnuts or garbanzo beans on a baking sheet until golden, about 8 minutes, watching carefully so that they do not burn. Remove and scrape into the bowl of a blender or food processor. Spread the sesame, coriander and cumin seeds over separate parts of the baking sheet, and roast until they are all colored and toasted, about 5 minutes. Remove and scrape them into the food processor bowl. Add salt and pepper to taste, the thyme, marjoram and lemon rind, if using. Let the nuts and seeds cool so that they are just warm before grinding; otherwise the nut oils will make the mixture too wet. Pulse briefly on and off until the mixture is roughly ground; do not overprocess. Serve with pieces of pocket bread. The nut mix will keep well for about one week if stored in an airtight container.

INGREDIENTS

½ CUP SHELLED HAZELNUTS OR
  ⅓ CUP SOAKED AND DRIED
  GARBANZO BEANS
¾ CUP SESAME SEEDS
¾ CUP CORIANDER SEEDS
⅔ CUP CUMIN SEEDS
SALT AND FRESHLY GROUND BLACK
  PEPPER
¼ TEASPOON DRIED THYME
¼ TEASPOON DRIED MARJORAM
DRIED LEMON RIND (OPTIONAL)

serves 4

Sweet Spiced Pistachios — LEBANON

INGREDIENTS

2½ CUPS SHELLED AND SALTED
    PISTACHIOS
¾ CUP GRANULATED SUGAR
1 TEASPOON GROUND MACE
1 TEASPOON GROUND CINNAMON

serves 4

METHOD

Place the nuts in a skillet without any oil, and heat until they are golden, stirring frequently; this will take about 4 to 5 minutes. Sprinkle over the sugar, then the spices, and continue to stir until the nuts have been caramelized. Take the nuts off the heat, and spoon onto foil or a baking sheet to dry. They will clump together, but if you wish, you can break them apart when dry. The nuts will keep for two weeks in an airtight container.

Avocado Cream Sauce — SPAIN

INGREDIENTS

1 LARGE RIPE AVOCADO
1 TABLESPOON LIME JUICE
⅔ CUP THICK SOUR CREAM OR CRÈME
    FRAÎCHE
1–2 TABLESPOONS CHOPPED FRESH
    CILANTRO

serves 8

A deliciously cool sauce, especially good with chili-based dishes.

METHOD

Halve the avocado, discard the pit, and scoop out the flesh. Mash, process or liquidize the avocado flesh with the remaining ingredients to make a thick cream. Serve as soon as possible. For a bit more bite, add 2 chopped scallions and/or ½ tablespoon of French mustard, and/or a few drops Tabasco. This is also good if you substitute ⅓ cup mayonnaise for the sour cream, especially if served with shrimp.

Curried Garbanzo Beans — INDIA

INGREDIENTS

GENEROUS 1 CUP GARBANZO BEANS,
    WASHED
3¾ CUPS WATER
4 TABLESPOONS OIL
PINCH OF ASAFETIDA
½ TEASPOON WHOLE CUMIN SEEDS
½ TEASPOON GROUND TURMERIC
½ TEASPOON CHILI POWDER
1 TEASPOON GROUND CORIANDER
1 TEASPOON GROUND CUMIN
1½ TEASPOON ARNCHOOR
½ TEASPOON SALT
2 TABLESPOONS LEMON JUICE, TO SERVE
1 TABLESPOON CHOPPED FRESH
    CILANTRO, TO GARNISH
1–2 FRESH GREEN CHILIES, CHOPPED, TO
    GARNISH

serves 4

METHOD

Soak the garbanzo beans in the water overnight. Boil the garbanzo beans with the water, cover and simmer for about 1 hour until tender. Drain and save the liquid. Heat the oil in a large saucepan over a medium heat, and add the asafetida and cumin seeds. Let them sizzle for a few seconds. Add the drained garbanzo beans, turmeric, chili powder, coriander, cumin, arnchoor, and salt, and stir-fry for 2 to 3 minutes. Add 1 cup of the bean stock, and cook for 20 minutes, stirring occasionally. Before serving, sprinkle with the lemon juice, cilantro leaves and green chilies.

Sweet spiced pistachios ▶

Homemade Tortilla Chips – MEXICO

INGREDIENTS

12 STALE TORTILLAS

⅓ CUP SALT (OPTIONAL)

OIL FOR DEEP-FRYING

serves 4 to 6

Sometimes, nothing but warm tortilla chips will do with homemade salsas. Fortunately they are not difficult to make. However, unless you have two large skillets, you'll be able to fry only a few tortilla chips at a time.

METHOD

To make the chips, cut stale tortillas into strips or wedges. (If the tortillas are fresh, dry them slightly by spreading them out and letting them sit for an hour or so.) If you want salted chips, make a brine of ⅓ cup salt and 2 cups of water. Briefly dip the tortilla pieces into the brine, then shake off the excess water. Pour ½ inch of vegetable oil into a large skillet and heat until the oil is hot but not smoking. Add the chips. If they are wet with brine, take care because the oil will splatter. Cook the chips until golden, turning once or twice, about 3 minutes, depending on how hot the oil is. Remove the chips from the oil, holding them briefly over the pan to drain off the excess oil, then place them on paper towels to drain thoroughly. Give the oil a few moments to reheat, then add a new batch of chips. A fat-free cooking alternative is to bake the chips. Preheat the oven to 325°F. Spread the prepared tortillas in a single layer on an ungreased baking sheet. Bake, turning occasionally, until they are crisp and lightly browned, about 40 minutes.

Hot Mixed Crushed Nuts — LEBANON

This is a thoroughly Lebanese version of mixed nuts, with a surprisingly spicy flavor. It is an acquired taste, but once acquired, often addictive.

METHOD

Crush the walnuts in batches with a mortar and pestle until they are in very small pieces. Follow with the pine nuts. Reserve. (Alternatively, chop the nuts with a sharp knife, using a rocking motion. Then use a rolling pin to crush the nuts more finely.) Warm the sunflower oil in a skillet to a medium heat. Add the garlic, chopped radishes and chilies. Sauté for several minutes, making sure the garlic does not burn. Add the nuts, and toss in the oil for 1 to 2 minutes, then stir in the scallions and the sesame oil. Stir for 1 minute, season to taste with cayenne pepper and salt, and transfer to a bowl to cool. Serve with pocket bread.

INGREDIENTS

1 CUP SHELLED WALNUTS, SKINNED

1 CUP SHELLED PINE NUTS

1 TABLESPOON SUNFLOWER OIL

1 GARLIC CLOVE, CRUSHED

10 RADISHES, TRIMMED AND FINELY CHOPPED

2 SMALL FRESH GREEN CHILIES, SEEDED AND FINELY CHOPPED

4 SCALLIONS, FINELY CHOPPED

½ TEASPOON SESAME OIL

PINCH OF CAYENNE PEPPER

PINCH OF SALT

serves 4

Green Plantain Chips – JAMAICA

INGREDIENTS

4 UNRIPE PLANTAINS

JUICE OF ½ LIME

PINCH OF SALT

VEGETABLE OIL FOR DEEP-FRYING

serves 6

METHOD

Peel the plantains, and rub them with the lime juice. Cut them into thin slices, and mix well with a pinch of salt. Heat some oil in a large skillet. Drain the plantain slices, then fry them for 3 minutes until they are crisp and golden brown. Remove them from the pan as they are ready, and drain them on paper towels. Serve when cool.

Oven-baked Florida Chips Two Ways – AMERICA

Here's a low-fat, low-calorie chip recipe. They are best served with salsa or chutney.

INGREDIENTS

2 EGG WHITES

1½ TABLESPOONS CHILI POWDER
 (FOR SPICY-HOT), OR ALLSPICE (FOR
 SPICY-SWEET)

4 BONIATOS, PEELED AND SLICED INTO
 THIN CHIPS

VEGETABLE OIL

SALT AND FRESHLY GROUND
 BLACK PEPPER

serves 4

METHOD

Preheat the oven to 450°F. In a large bowl, lightly beat the egg whites with a fork until foamy. Stir in either the chili powder or allspice. Add the boniatos, and toss to coat well.

Spread the chips in a single layer on a lightly oiled baking sheet. Bake for 30 to 35 minutes, or until the potatoes are crisp and browned. Season to taste.

Fresh Salsa – MEXICO

"Salsa" literally means "sauce," but in the absence of other qualifications it normally means salsa cruda, "raw sauce," which appears on the table as regularly as pepper and salt. It is frequently used as a dip, with corn chips, but it can be spooned onto almost any savory dish such as omelets, or meat . . . you name it. Most salsas crudas improve and mature if left overnight in the refrigerator. The basic ingredients, mixed-and-matched in a wide variety of combinations, are dried or fresh chili peppers; onions; tomatoes (including tomatillos); garlic and cilantro. Optional additions include oregano, vinegar and olive oil.

METHOD

Wash the cilantro and remove the coarser stems and roots. A gringo might use as little as a teaspoon of chopped cilantro; a Mexican would probably use half a bunch – about a handful, before chopping. Chop the onion and tomatoes finely, the garlic, chilies and cilantro very finely. Put them all in a large bowl. Squish them together with your hand, squeezing and rubbing to blend and increase flavour. You can also use a food processor. Chop the garlic and chili first; then add the onion, and chop some more; then add the rest. The traditional way to make it is to grind the ingredients together in a pestle and mortar.

Salsa Variations

Roast one or two poblano or Anaheim chillies over an open flame; when they are charred all over, remove the skin. Remove the seeds, and veins, chop and add to the salsa. Use fresh tomatoes instead of canned: either peel them (dip in boiling water for 10 to 30 seconds) or leave the skins on. Remove the tomato seeds, or not, as you feel inclined. For a thicker salsa, use a can of crushed tomatoes with added tomato paste. If you like, add any of the following: a pinch of oregano and/or a tablespoon of olive oil. Fresh coriander seeds are a wonderful addition to salsa – a strong argument for growing your own. In the absence of fresh serrano chilies, shred a dried red chili and grind it in a little water with the garlic; let soak for a while; and add this paste to the tomato, onion and cilantro. For a rock-bottom-basic dipping salsa, add the same chili/garlic paste to half a can of commercial tomato sauce.

INGREDIENTS

SMALL HANDFUL OF FRESH CILANTRO

1 LARGE ONION, RED OR WHITE

1½ POUNDS CANNED TOMATOES

1-4 GARLIC CLOVES

2 FRESH SERRANO CHILIES, OR

   1 JALAPEÑO

serves 8

Tomato Chili Sauce – THAILAND

METHOD

Split and seed the chilies, and slice thinly. Fry the onion and garlic in the oil until just beginning to brown. Turn down the heat, add the chilies, and cook, covered, until the onions have softened, about 12 minutes. Add the tomato paste, oregano, paprika, sugar, and water or wine, and simmer for 7 to 10 minutes longer, until the sauce has thickened slightly. Add salt to taste. Serve hot or cold.

INGREDIENTS

3–4 FRESH RED CHILIES

2 MEDIUM ONIONS, CHOPPED

2 GARLIC CLOVES, CRUSHED

2 TABLESPOONS OLIVE OIL

3 TABLESPOONS TOMATO PASTE

1 TEASPOON DRIED OREGANO

2 TEASPOONS PAPRIKA

1 TEASPOON SUGAR

½ CUP WATER OR RED WINE

PINCH OF SALT

serves 4

Sofrito – CUBA

Sofrito comes from the Spanish verb meaning "to sauté." This thick tomato-pepper salsa is also a staple in Cuban kitchens. Complements chicken and rice dishes, Basque-style cod dishes and omelets, or use it to spread on tortillas.

INGREDIENTS

2 ONIONS, FINELY CHOPPED
1 LARGE GREEN BELL PEPPER, SEEDED
   AND DICED
5 GARLIC CLOVES, MASHED
½ CUP OLIVE OIL
1 x 4-OUNCE JAR DICED
   PIMENTOS, DRAINED
8-OUNCE CAN TOMATO SAUCE
1 TEASPOON DRIED OREGANO
1 TABLESPOON RED WINE VINEGAR

serves 4

METHOD

In a large pan over low heat, sauté the onions, green bell pepper and garlic in the olive oil until tender and lightly browned, for about 15 minutes. Add the pimentos and cook for 5 more minutes over low heat. Add the tomato sauce, oregano and vinegar and cook 10 more minutes. Let cool, then store in tightly closed jar in refrigerator for up to two weeks.

Salsa Cruda – MEXICO

This salsa uses the hotter serrano chilies. It is an all-purpose salsa, good with corn chips, over tacos and tostadas, with meat and fish, or mixed into rice.

INGREDIENTS

4 MEDIUM TOMATOES, CORED AND
   HALVED
1 CUP CHOPPED ONION
5 FRESH SERRANO CHILIES,
   PARTLY SEEDED IF DESIRED, MINCED
2 GARLIC CLOVES, CRUSHED
3 TABLESPOONS FRESH CILANTRO,
   CHOPPED
2 TABLESPOONS LIME JUICE
1 TABLESPOON OLIVE OIL
¼ – ½ TEASPOON SALT

serves 4

METHOD

Cut the tomatoes in half, and squeeze out the seeds. Broil the tomatoes cut side down on a flameproof baking sheet until the skins are partly blackened and slip off easily. Remove from heat. Let them cool in a colander so excess liquids drain off, and then remove the skins. Purée in a blender or food processor, but do not purée so long that the tomato becomes liquefied. Stir all the remaining ingredients together, and add the tomatoes. Let stand for 30 minutes, then taste and adjust the seasoning.

Sofrito ▶

Chorizo-Bean Dip — MEXICO

INGREDIENTS

1 CUP DRIED BLACK BEANS

5 OUNCES CHORIZO SAUSAGE

½ CUP CHOPPED ONION

1–2 TEASPOONS SALT

¾ CUP SALSA CRUDA (PAGE 20)

serves 8

Black beans puréed with spicy chorizo sausage and salsa make a delicious hot dip for corn chips. The leftovers are so good in omelets, empanadas, and tostaditas that you'll want to make a double batch.

METHOD

Sort through the beans, and discard any pebbles or other debris. Soak the beans overnight in 4 cups water, or bring the beans and water to a boil and boil for 2 minutes, then turn off the heat and let stand, covered, for 1 hour. Drain and rinse the beans. Put the beans in a medium saucepan with 4 cups water. Bring to a boil, reduce the heat and simmer. Crumble the chorizo into a small skillet and fry until browned, 5 to 7 minutes. Tilt the pan to drain the grease, remove the meat with a slotted spoon, and add to the beans. Discard all but 1 tablespoon grease in the pan. Reheat, and add the chopped onion. Sauté for 5 minutes, then add to the beans. Continue simmering the beans until tender, adding a little more water, if needed, so that there is still some cooking liquid left when the beans are done. The total cooking time should be 1 to 1½ hours. Stir in 1 teaspoon salt. Remove the pan from the heat, and set aside about ½ cup beans. Purée the rest in a blender or food processor, then stir in the whole beans and the salsa. Taste and add more salt if necessary. Serve warm.

Hummus – MIDDLE EAST

This creamy, golden purée of garbanzo beans is a specialty of Middle Eastern Jews and non-Jews alike. It is popular as an appetizer or one of many dishes in a *meze* of Middle Eastern food. It is worth
making a large batch of hummus as it keeps well in the refrigerator, and is ideal to serve when

METHOD

Rinse the dried garbanzo beans very well, discarding any broken or discolored ones. Place in a large bowl, and cover generously with cold water; soak for 12 hours or overnight. Transfer the beans and their soaking water to a large stockpot, and, over medium heat, bring to a boil. Reduce heat and let simmer for 1½ to 2 hours, until very tender. Add 1 teaspoon salt and continue simmering for 30 minutes. Drain well, reserving 1 tablespoon of the beans and a little cooking liquid. Press cooked or canned beans through a food mill or strainer, adding reserved cooking liquid, to separate beans from skins. (For a smooth hummus, skins must be separated from beans.) Discard skins. Process crushed garlic with a pinch of salt in a blender or food processor. Add puréed beans and process until smooth. Add the lemon juice, tahini, and a pinch of cayenne pepper, and purée until finely blended. Hummus should be thick and smooth; add a little more cooking liquid if purée is too thick, and adjust the seasoning. Transfer to a bowl and store in the refrigerator, covered, for up to five days. To serve, spread hummus in a shallow dish or individual bowls, and with the back of a spoon make a hollow in the center. Chop the reserved beans coarsely and sprinkle over. If wished, pour a little olive oil in the center of the well, garnish with the chopped beans, parsley and a sprinkling of cayenne pepper.

INGREDIENTS

1 POUND DRIED GARBANZO BEANS, OR 2 CANS, WELL RINSED

SALT

4–6 GARLIC CLOVES, PEELED AND CRUSHED

¼ CUP LEMON JUICE

¼ CUP TAHINI

CAYENNE PEPPER

OLIVE OIL AND FRESH PARSLEY, CHOPPED, TO GARNISH

serves 8 to 10

Spicy Meat and Tomato Dip – THAILAND

This is a relatively mild dip, and in northern Thai fashion, guests eat from the bowl in which it is served, scooping with the pork rind, vegetables or sticky rice.

METHOD

Pound the chilies, onion, lemon grass, garlic, shrimp paste, and salt together with a mortar and pestle or in a blender or food processor until fine. Heat the oil in a wok or pan, and add the chili mixture, the pork, and tomatoes. Cook until thick, about 15 minutes, then add the water, and cook again for 10 minutes until thick. Adjust the seasoning to taste with lemon juice, Nuoc Mam sauce and/or sugar. Garnish with the cilantro leaves. Serve accompanied by raw or slightly cooked vegetables, sticky rice, and if you can buy it, crispy pork rind (often sold under the Spanish name "chicharrones").

INGREDIENTS

6 DRIED RED CHILIES, CHOPPED

3 TABLESPOONS CHOPPED SHALLOTS

1 TABLESPOON SLICED LEMON GRASS

1 TABLESPOON CHOPPED GARLIC

2 TEASPOONS SHRIMP PASTE

2 TEASPOONS SALT

2 TABLESPOONS PEANUT OR CORN OIL

⅔ CUP CHOPPED RAW PORK

8 CHERRY TOMATOES, DICED

½ CUP WATER

DASH OF LEMON JUICE, TO TASTE

DASH OF NUOC MAM SAUCE TO TASTE OR A DASH OF LIGHT SOY SAUCE WITH A DASH OF ANCHOVY ESSENCE

PINCH OF SUGAR

½ CUP FRESH CILANTRO, TO GARNISH

serves 4 to 6

Red Chili Sauce — MEXICO

INGREDIENTS

12 DRIED NEW MEXICO CHILIES

2½ CUPS BEEF STOCK

4 GARLIC CLOVES, CRUSHED

½ CUP CHOPPED ONION

½ TEASPOON DRIED OREGANO

¼ TEASPOON SALT

serves 8

This hot chili sauce is used most often to make enchiladas, but it can be added to meat or beans, or served as a table sauce to be spooned over tacos, eggs, or other dishes. For less heat, substitute dried California chilies for some of the New Mexico chilies.

METHOD

Preheat the oven to 250°F. Place the chilies on an ungreased baking sheet, and bake for 6 to 8 minutes, shaking once or twice, until they are brittle. Do not let them blacken, or they will be bitter. Remove the chilies, and let stand until they are cool enough to handle. Remove the stems and as many of the seeds as liked. Bring 4 cups water to a boil in a medium saucepan. Crumble the chilies into the boiling water, and simmer for 20 to 30 minutes until soft. Drain off the water and discard. Put the chilies into a blender or food processor with about 6 tablespoons of the beefstock and purée. Strain to remove the skins. Put the skins back in the blender with another 6 tablespoons beef stock. Purée again and strain. Discard the skins. Add the remaining ingredients to the strained sauce and purée. Return the sauce to the heat, and simmer until it reaches the desired consistency.

Avocado Bi Tahini — LEBANON

INGREDIENTS

2 GARLIC CLOVES, CRUSHED

PINCH OF SALT

2 RIPE AVOCADOS

JUICE OF 2 LEMONS

5 TABLESPOONS TAHINI PASTE

1 TEASPOON GROUND CUMIN

CRUSHED DRIED RED CHILIES,

    TO GARNISH

serves 4 to 6

This is a standard *meze* dip where ripe avocados flood the markets in Lebanon, though it is less frequently encountered in Lebanese restaurants abroad. It is particularly simple to make.

METHOD

In a bowl, mash the garlic with salt to taste. Cut the avocados in half, take out the pit and scoop the flesh into the bowl. Mash together with salt, garlic, and a little of the lemon juice, until there are no lumps. Whip in the remaining lemon juice, the tahini and the ground cumin. Beat to a smooth purée. Transfer the purée into a bowl, swirl the top decoratively, and rub a few crushed chili peppers between the fingers to sprinkle over the top. Serve with warm pocket bread.

Florida-style Smoky Fish Pâté — AMERICA

INGREDIENTS

1 POUND SMOKED MARLIN

⅔ CUP SWEET PICKLE RELISH

¼ CUP PREPARED HORSERADISH SAUCE

1 SMALL ONION, CHOPPED

1 CELERY STALK, PEELED AND FINELY

    CHOPPED

½ TEASPOON LIME JUICE

1 TEASPOON TABASCO SAUCE

⅓ CUP MAYONNAISE

SALT AND GROUND BLACK PEPPER

serves 6 to 8

You may use any smoked fish for this tangy pâté. Serve with an assortment of crackers.

METHOD

Coarsely chop the fish, and place in a mixing bowl. Add the relish, horseradish, onion, celery, and lime juice, and mix well. Add half of the Tabasco sauce and half the mayonnaise. Blend together and taste. Add more Tabasco, according to your taste. Add more mayonnaise, and mix until the desired texture and taste is achieved.

Florida-style smoky fish pâté ▶

Shrimp Butter – AMERICA

This easy hors d'oeuvre spread can be made ahead of time and brought to room temperature just before serving. Spread the shrimp butter on crackers or miniature toasts.

INGREDIENTS

8 OUNCES COOKED AND CLEANED
  SHRIMP, ANY SIZE
½ CUP BUTTER AT ROOM TEMPERATURE
2 TABLESPOONS FINELY CHOPPED
  SCALLIONS
1 TEASPOON CAPERS, DRAINED
2 TEASPOONS LEMON JUICE
½ TEASPOON FRESH HORSERADISH,
  GRATED
¼ TEASPOON SALT
⅛ TEASPOON CAYENNE PEPPER
FRESHLY GROUND PEPPER

serves 12

METHOD
Put all the ingredients in blender or food processor and process until smooth.

Yogurt Cream Cheese Dip – LEBANON

Usually made with goats' milk yogurt in Lebanon, this mild but flavorful cream cheese dip is ubiquitous on the Lebanese table. It is a popular *meze* dip, and can be turned into a more substantial variation by the addition of one or more of the following ingredients: chopped cucumber, scallions, sweet bell peppers or chilies.

INGREDIENTS

4 CUPS PLAIN YOGURT (GOAT OR
  SHEEP PREFERRED)
1 TEASPOON SALT
1 TABLESPOON OLIVE OIL
PINCH OF PAPRIKA

serves 4 to 6

METHOD
In a bowl, combine the yogurt and the salt, and whip to mix thoroughly. Line a strainer with damp cheesecloth or a clean, fine-weave cloth. Let it drain in this position for a while; then tie the corners of the cloth together, and hang it from a faucet over the sink for about 12 hours or overnight. To serve, decant the drained cheese into a bowl. Swirl the top decoratively, and drizzle the olive oil over the cheese. Sprinkle with the paprika. Serve with warm pocket bread.

Tzatziki – GREECE

This light and refreshing dip should always be served well chilled. On its own with fresh pocket bread or as an accompaniment to fritters and other fried foods, it is easy to make and very delicious.

METHOD

Place the yogurt in a medium sized bowl. Peel and grate the cucumber, squeezing a little at a time in the palm of your hand to remove the excess water. Stir the cucumber into the yogurt.

Stir in the garlic, fresh mint, olive oil and vinegar and season to taste. Just before serving, garnish with chopped fresh mint.

INGREDIENTS

1 POUND NATURAL YOGURT

½ CUCUMBER

3 GARLIC CLOVES, CRUSHED

2 TABLESPOONS CHOPPED FRESH MINT

2 TABLESPOONS OLIVE OIL

1 TABLESPOON WHITE WINE VINEGAR

PINCH OF SALT

CHOPPED FRESH MINT, TO GARNISH

serves 4 to 6

Green Chili Dip – THAILAND

High on the scale of chili "heat," but green and fresh-tasting. Intended to be eaten with sticky rice and assorted raw vegetables, and as part of a larger meal. Traditionally, everyone eats from one central bowl.

METHOD

Fry the dried fish in the oil over medium heat for about 7 to 10 minutes and drain. Dry-fry the chilies, garlic, shallots and tomatoes until fragrant, about 8 to 10 minutes. Place in a bowl. Pound them lightly with the dry fish. Add the water, scallion, and cilantro, and mix well.

Taste to check: it should be of a sauce consistency and a touch salty; if not, add more water or Nuoc Mam sauce as required. Serve accompanied by raw cabbage wedges, sliced cucumbers, raw green beans and/or fried or roasted fish.

INGREDIENTS

1 TABLESPOON DRIED SALTED MACKEREL
   OR ANCHOVY, CHOPPED

4 TABLESPOONS PEANUT OR CORN OIL

10 FRESH 2-INCH GREEN CHILIES,
   COARSELY CHOPPED

10 GARLIC CLOVES, COARSELY CHOPPED

6 SHALLOTS, COARSELY CHOPPED

3 CHERRY TOMATOES

2 TABLESPOONS HOT WATER

1 TABLESPOON SCALLIONS, CHOPPED

1 TABLESPOON CHOPPED FRESH
   CILANTRO

DASH OF NUOC MAM SAUCE OR A
   DASH OF LIGHT SOY SAUCE WITH A
   DASH OF ANCHOVY SAUCE

serves 6

Smoked Grouper Spread – AMERICA

INGREDIENTS

7 OUNCES COOKED GROUPER, BONES
    AND SKIN REMOVED

1 CUP SOFTENED CREAM CHEESE

1 TABLESPOON LIME JUICE

1 TABLESPOON GRATED ONION

1 TEASPOON PREPARED HORSERADISH
    SAUCE

¼ TEASPOON LIQUID SMOKE

½ CUP CHOPPED WALNUTS

3 TABLESPOONS FRESH PARSLEY OR
    CILANTRO

serves 4

Grouper spread is popular at many bars in South Florida where it is usually eaten on crackers. It also makes a nifty dip for crudités, too. Any white-fleshed fillet, such as halibut, whitefish or snapper, can be substituted, or, at a pinch, use drained canned pink salmon.

METHOD

Combine the grouper, cream cheese, lime juice, onion, horseradish, and liquid smoke in a blender or food processor. Process until smooth.

Stir in the walnuts and parsley or cilantro. Transfer to a heavy small bowl. Cover and refrigerate until ready to serve.

Vodka Dip – AMERICA

INGREDIENTS

1 CUP MAYONNAISE

1 TABLESPOON TOMATO PASTE

4 TABLESPOONS VODKA

12 SCALLIONS, CHOPPED

4 TABLESPOONS CHOPPED FRESH
    PARSLEY

2 TABLESPOONS LEMON JUICE

1 TEASPOON GROUND CUMIN

DASH OF TABASCO SAUCE

serves 4

METHOD

In a small bowl, whisk the mayonnaise with the tomato paste, then whisk in the remaining ingredients. Cover and refrigerate for at least 3 hours or overnight. Serve with Malanga Pancakes (page 73).

Seafood Salsa Spread — MEXICO

This simple spread is made by combining salsa and seafood, then pouring it over a block of cream cheese. Use a tomato-based salsa of your choice, but it should be a cooked salsa or one made with broiled tomatoes, as raw tomatoes will exude watery juice. Serve with crackers or raw vegetables.

METHOD
Mix the salsa and shrimp or crab meat. Place the cream cheese on a serving dish, and pour the salsa over the top.

INGREDIENTS
¼ CUP TOMATO-BASED SALSA

ABOUT ⅔ CUP TINY COOKED SHRIMP
OR CRAB MEAT

8-OUNCE PACKAGE CREAM CHEESE

serves 4 to 6

Mia-Mex Star Fruit and Black Bean Salsa — AMERICA

INGREDIENTS

1 X 8-OUNCE CAN BLACK
    BEANS, DRAINED

½ CUP CORN KERNELS, FRESH, FROZEN
    OR CANNED AND DRAINED

1¼ CUPS CHOPPED RIPE TOMATOES

4 SCALLIONS, TRIMMED AND
    CHOPPED

½ GREEN BELL PEPPER, SEEDED AND
    FINELY DICED

½ RED BELL PEPPER, SEEDED AND
    FINELY DICED

2 TABLESPOONS OLIVE OIL

½ CUP RED WINE VINEGAR

DASH OF TABASCO SAUCE

DASH OF WORCESTERSHIRE SAUCE

PINCH OF GROUND CUMIN

SALT AND FRESHLY GROUND
    BLACK PEPPER

1 STAR FRUIT, ½ SLICED CROSSWISE IN
    THIN SECTIONS, ½ DICED

serves 4 to 6

METHOD

Mix the beans with the corn, tomatoes, onions, bell peppers, olive oil, and vinegar, and season to taste with the Tabasco sauce, Worcestershire sauce, cumin, salt, and pepper. Stir the diced star fruit slices into the mixture, and place the others across the top. Cover and refrigerate for at least 3 hours to let flavors blend, then serve chilled.

Ewes' Cheese with Paprika — POLAND

INGREDIENTS

4 OUNCES EWES' CHEESE

6 TABLESPOONS SOUR CREAM

½ TEASPOON PAPRIKA

1 TABLESPOON CHIVES, SNIPPED

serves 4

This spread is good with rye bread or it may be used on canapés. Try healthfood stores for ewes' cheese, or use a good feta cheese instead.

METHOD

Mash the cheese with a fork, then gradually work in the sour cream to make a smooth paste. Stir in the paprika and chives. Chill lightly before serving with rye bread.

Mia-mex star fruit and black bean salsa ▶

Chopped Liver – ISRAEL

INGREDIENTS

1 POUND CHICKEN LIVERS

PINCH OF SALT

PINCH OF FRESHLY GROUND
   BLACK PEPPER

2 TABLESPOONS VEGETABLE OIL

2 MEDIUM ONIONS, CHOPPED

4 HARD-COOKED EGGS, CHOPPED

CHICKEN STOCK (OPTIONAL)

SHREDDED LETTUCE, TO GARNISH

CHERRY TOMATOES, TO GARNISH

serves 6 to 8

This is probably the best-known and best-loved Jewish dish. No one really knows its origins, but when it comes to chopped liver, everybody's an expert. Traditionally, chicken fat is used to cook the onions and bind the mixture, as well as provide a smooth texture. This version replaces the fat with vegetable oil which is less rich and lower in saturated fat. Use a kosher margarine if you prefer. Serve with rye bread, chalah or matzo. For an elegant presentation, pipe onto toast or crackers.

METHOD

Preheat the broiler. Arrange the livers on a foil-lined broiler pan, and sprinkle with salt. Broil until lightly brown, 3 to 4 minutes. Turn the livers over, sprinkle with salt, and broil until just cooked through, 3 to 4 minutes longer; livers should no longer be pink. Remove the livers to a cooling rack to drain and cool slightly. Heat the oil in a large skillet, over a medium heat. Add the chopped onions, and cook until soft and golden, 10 to 12 minutes, stirring occasionally.

In a blender or food processor, chop the livers coarsely using the pulse action. Add the onions and, using the pulse action, chop until livers and onions are just blended. Add the chopped eggs, salt and pepper to taste, and chop again until just blended. If the mixture is dry, add a little more oil or a spoonful of chicken stock. Spoon the mixture into a serving bowl, cover and refrigerate for 2 hours, or until ready to serve. Garnish with shredded lettuce and cherry tomatoes.

Shrimp Salsa – AMERICA

INGREDIENTS

2 MEDIUM TOMATOES, SEEDED AND
    CHOPPED

½ CUCUMBER, PEELED, SEEDED AND
    DICED

3 SCALLIONS, FINELY CHOPPED

1 MILD FRESH CHILI, SEEDED AND FINELY
    CHOPPED

2 TABLESPOONS CHOPPED FRESH
    CILANTRO

1½ TABLESPOONS OLIVE OIL

1½ TABLESPOONS CIDER VINEGAR

PINCH OF SALT

DASH OF TABASCO SAUCE

¾ CUP TINY BROWN SHRIMP, COOKED
    AND CLEANED

serves 4

A cool, easy dip for crackers, chips or vegetables. Make a couple of hours ahead to let the flavors blend. Taste again just before serving, and adjust the Tabasco sauce.

METHOD
Combine all the ingredients in a bowl, and refrigerate for at least 2 hours before serving.

Cottage Cheese Spread – POLAND

Although Polish cottage cheese has a bland flavor similar to the cottage cheese we buy in tubs, it is white and firm enough to cut into crumbly slices. Serve this simple spread with rye bread, or use it as a topping for canapés.

METHOD
Spoon the cottage cheese onto a double thick piece of scalded cheesecloth. Gather up the ends of the cloth, and twist them together to squeeze as much liquid as possible from it. Put the cheese in a bowl, using a spatula to scrape all the dry curds off the cheesecloth, and mash it with a fork. Stir in the sour cream, pickled cucumber and dill, adding seasoning to taste. Spoon the mixture into a serving dish, and chill for about 30 minutes. Garnish with dill, if liked, before serving.

INGREDIENTS

1½ CUPS COTTAGE CHEESE

4 TABLESPOONS SOUR CREAM

1 PICKLED CUCUMBER, DICED

1 TABLESPOON CHOPPED FRESH DILL

SALT AND FRESHLY GROUND
    BLACK PEPPER

DILL SPRIGS, TO GARNISH

serves 4

Black-eyed Pea Dip — AMERICA

Ham, crunchy vegetables and liberal use of Tabasco sauce turn the humble black-eyed pea into a tasty dip. If you're a fan of spicy food, add finely chopped jalapeño chili to the recipe. The dip is traditionally served with sesame crackers, but it's good with vegetable crudités too.

INGREDIENTS

6 OUNCES DRIED BLACK-EYED PEAS

1 LARGE OR 2 PORK KNUCKLES

1 MEDIUM ONION, CUT INTO CHUNKS

1 DRIED RED CHILI PEPPER

1 CUP SOUR CREAM

1 TEASPOON SALT

¼ TEASPOON BLACK PEPPER

2 OUNCES CHOPPED SCALLION

2 OUNCES CHOPPED GREEN OR RED BELL
   PEPPER

DASH OF TABASCO SAUCE

serves 4

METHOD

Soak peas overnight. Drain. Place in medium saucepan with pork, onion and dried pepper. Add enough water to cover. Bring to a boil, then simmer until peas are tender, about 1 hour, adding water if needed. Drain the peas, reserving about ½ cup liquid and the pork. Discard the onion and dried pepper. Purée the peas in a blender or food processor, adding the cooking liquid a tablespoon at a time, until the mixture is still a little dry but almost smooth, probably 4 to 6 tablespoons. Add the sour cream. Cut the meat from the pork, discard the fatty parts, and finely chop the meat. Add it to the purée with the salt and black pepper. Just before serving, add the onion, green or red bell pepper, and Tabasco sauce to taste.

Mushroom Caviar — RUSSIAN FEDERATION

Eastern Europeans, particularly Russians and Poles, are mushroom fanatics. Dawn expeditions into the wooded countryside in search of fungi are a common sight in the fall.

INGREDIENTS

4 CUPS FINELY CHOPPED FRESH
   MUSHROOMS (THE MORE VARIETIES,
   THE BETTER — FIELD, SHIITAKE,
   OYSTER, GIROLLE, ETC)

1 FINELY CHOPPED MEDIUM ONION

½ CUP BUTTER

1 TABLESPOON DRY SHERRY

⅓ CUP SMOOTH COTTAGE CHEESE

⅓ CUP CREAM CHEESE

1 CUP FINELY CHOPPED FRESH PARSLEY

½ CUP FINELY CHOPPED FRESH
   TARRAGON

½ CUP FINELY CHOPPED FRESH
   MARJORAM

serves 8 to 10

METHOD

In a large skillet, sauté the mushrooms and onion in the butter over medium heat, stirring often. When the mushrooms are browned and softened, add the sherry. Remove from the heat. In a bowl, beat together the two cheeses and the finely chopped herbs. Stir in the mushrooms, onion and their juices. Beat the mixture with a wooden spoon until it is well combined. Spoon the pâté into a small china dish, smooth, swirl the top and cover. Chill overnight or up to three days before serving with small rye rounds.

Cold

Bites

~

Haminados – ISRAEL

These slow-cooked eggs are a typical Sephardic Passover dish. They are sometimes cooked in a stew, such as hamin or dfina, but are simple to do on their own. Serve as an appetizer, sliced in salads, or at barbecues or picnics with hummus. The onion skins give the eggs their golden brown color.

INGREDIENTS

8 LARGE EGGS

SKINS OF 8 ONIONS

1 TEASPOON SALT

½ TEASPOON FRESHLY GROUND BLACK PEPPER

2 TABLESPOONS OLIVE OIL

serves 4 to 8

METHOD

Preheat the oven to 350°F. Place all the ingredients in a small ovenproof casserole, and add enough water to cover. Cover tightly and place in the oven. Immediately reduce the heat to 200°F, and bake for 6 to 8 hours or overnight. Rinse and drain the eggs. They can be served warm or chilled with a little hummus on the side.

Eggs à la Russe – RUSSIAN FEDERATION

While the origins of this dish lie within the borders of the Austro-Hungarian rather than the Russian Empire – it was a favorite of turn-of-the-century Viennese chefs – the marriage of ingredients justifies the name they gave it.

INGREDIENTS

6 HARD-COOKED EGGS, HALVED

2 TABLESPOONS MAYONNAISE

½ TEASPOON DRY MUSTARD POWDER

1 TABLESPOON DIJON MUSTARD

3 TABLESPOONS FINELY CHOPPED SOUR-SWEET GHERKINS

2 TEASPOONS FINELY CHOPPED SCALLIONS

SALT AND BLACK PEPPER

CAPERS, TO GARNISH

PAPRIKA, TO GARNISH

serves 6

METHOD

Remove the yolks from the halved eggs, reserving the whites, and place them in a small bowl. Mash them thoroughly, then blend the mayonnaise, the two mustards, the chopped gherkins, and scallion, and season to taste. Spoon the mixture into the egg-white halves, and garnish decoratively with the capers and paprika.

Minsk-style Eggs – BELORUSSIA

These eggs make a frequent appearance at Christmas and Easter festivities in Russia. They are traditionally eaten warm, with horn spoons, but they are also good cold.

INGREDIENTS

10 HARD-COOKED EGGS

⅓ CUP SOFTENED, UNSALTED BUTTER

1 TABLESPOON MAYONNAISE

2 TABLESPOONS HEAVY CREAM

3½ TABLESPOONS FRESH DILL

2 TEASPOONS SWEET PAPRIKA

1 TABLESPOON PARSLEY, CHOPPED

4 TABLESPOONS DRY BREAD CRUMBS

3 TABLESPOONS GRATED GRUYÈRE
    CHEESE

16 ANCHOVY FILLETS, RINSED, DRIED
    AND CUT IN HALF LENGTHWAYS

FRESH WATERCRESS SPRIGS, TO GARNISH

serves 8

METHOD

Halve the eggs, and carefully remove the yolks. Set aside the sixteen best whites. In a bowl, mash the yolks well with the softened butter. Beat in the mayonnaise, cream, dill, paprika, parsley, and seasoning to taste. Finely chop the four extra whites, and stir them into the mixture. Divide the filling between the sixteen reserved egg whites. Preheat the oven to 400°. Place the filled eggs on a baking sheet. Mix the bread crumbs and grated cheese together, and sprinkle evenly over the yolks. Cross each egg with two strips of anchovy to make an "X." Bake for 10 minutes, until the eggs are warmed through and the tops are golden. Arrange sprigs of watercress on eight plates, and put two egg-halves on each plate. Serve warm.

Tea Eggs – CHINA

INGREDIENTS

12 EGGS

2 TEASPOONS SALT

3 TABLESPOONS LIGHT SOY SAUCE

2 TABLESPOONS DARK SOY SAUCE

1 TEASPOON FIVE-SPICE POWDER

1 TABLESPOON RED TEA LEAVES

serves 12

METHOD

Boil the eggs in water for 5 to 10 minutes. Remove and gently tap the shell of each egg with a spoon until it is cracked finely all over. Place the eggs back in the pan, and cover with fresh water. Add the salt, soy sauces, five-spice powder, and tea leaves (the better the quality of the tea, the better the result). Bring to a boil and simmer for 30 to 40 minutes. Let the eggs cool in the liquid. Peel off the shells – the eggs will have a beautiful marbled pattern. They can be served either on their own, or as part of a mixed hors d'oeuvre, whole or cut into halves or quarters.

Anchovy and Egg Fritters – EGYPT

Eggah, as it is known in Egypt where it is particularly popular, occurs in a number of guises throughout the region. A form of omelet, it is sometimes made with flour in Lebanon, becoming a *beignet.* Here it is extended with potato and cut into wedges.

INGREDIENTS

2 TABLESPOONS OLIVE OR SUNFLOWER
   OIL

5 SCALLIONS, FINELY CHOPPED

6 ANCHOVIES, WASHED, DRAINED,
   DRIED AND FINELY CHOPPED

1 LARGE POTATO, GRATED

1 TEASPOON CUMIN

3 TABLESPOONS FINELY CHOPPED FLAT-
   LEAFED PARSLEY

6 EGGS

SALT AND FRESHLY GROUND
   BLACK PEPPER

serves 4 to 6

METHOD

Heat the oil in a large skillet with a cover. When hot, add the chopped scallions and sauté until they are limp. Take off the heat and transfer the scallions with a slotted spoon to a large bowl. Add the chopped anchovies, grated potato, cumin, and parsley to the bowl, and mix together. One by one, beat in the eggs. Season according to taste. Put the pan back on the heat, turning to coat it with the oil. Pour in the egg mixture, turn the heat to low, and cover. Cook for about 15 to 20 minutes, until the eggs are just set. Uncover the pan, put a plate over the top, and invert the flat omelet onto the plate. Carefully slip it back into the pan and cook for 3 minutes longer. Remove the omelet, cut into thin wedges, and roll up each wedge, fat end to thin point of the triangle. Secure with a toothpick. Serve warm or cold.

Cajun Deviled Eggs – AMERICA

INGREDIENTS

6 HARD-COOKED EGGS

¼ CUP FINELY CHOPPED TASSO

1 TABLESPOON FINELY CHOPPED GREEN
   BELL PEPPER

1 SCALLION, FINELY CHOPPED

½ TEASPOON LEMON JUICE

2 TABLESPOONS MAYONNAISE

2 TABLESPOONS DIJON MUSTARD

PINCH OF FRESHLY GROUND
   BLACK PEPPER

DASH OF TABASCO SAUCE

serves 3 to 6

The tasso gives these deviled eggs their spicy taste. If you don't have tasso, use another ham, but add cayenne pepper and paprika to give it a Cajun flavor.

METHOD

Cut the eggs in half lengthways. Remove the yolks, and put them in a small bowl. Set the whites aside. Mash the yolks with a fork. Add the remaining ingredients to the yolks, and mix well with a fork. Taste and adjust the seasonings. Spoon the mixture into the egg whites.

Chili Manchego – SPAIN

INGREDIENTS

6 FRESH RED CHILIES, SEEDED AND
   CHOPPED

1 CUP OLIVE OIL

SALT AND FRESHLY GROUND
   BLACK PEPPER

1 POUND MANCHEGO CHEESE

serves 4

This is a spicy *tapa* – serve it with plenty of crusty bread, a wedge of lime and ice-cold beer.

METHOD

Blend the chilies with the olive oil, adding a good pinch each of salt and pepper. Cut the cheese into small, "spikable" cubes. Pour the oil over the cheese, and marinate for at least 2 hours before serving.

Cajun deviled eggs ▶

Crunchy Fried Shrimp Canapés with Gingery Mayonnaise — AMERICA

INGREDIENTS

1½ PINTS COOKED SHRIMP, SHELLED
 AND DEVEINED

ALL-PURPOSE FLOUR SEASONED WITH
 SALT AND CAYENNE PEPPER

VEGETABLE OIL FOR DEEP-FRYING

2 TABLESPOONS PEELED AND MINCED
 GINGER ROOT

⅔ CUP MAYONNAISE

3 TABLESPOONS DIJON MUSTARD

4 SLICES RYE BREAD, CUT INTO
 2-INCH ROUNDS AND TOASTED
 LIGHTLY

10 RADISHES, TRIMMED AND THINLY
 SLICED

½ CUP ALFALFA SPROUTS

WATERCRESS OR CILANTRO, TO GARNISH
 (OPTIONAL)

2 TEASPOONS LEMON JUICE

serves 4 to 6

An array of textures and colors and the ginger-scented shrimp make this appetizer one for special occasions. These are nice to pass round with cocktails, or with aperitifs before a dinner party because they are not too filling.

METHOD

Toss the shrimp with seasoned flour in a bag to coat them. Transfer them to a strainer, and shake off the excess flour. Heat 1 inch of oil over moderately high heat until it registers 375°F on a deep-fat thermometer, and fry the shrimp in batches, stirring occasionally, for 1 minute, or until they are just cooked through. Transfer them to paper towels to drain. In a small bowl, stir together the ginger root, mayonnaise, and mustard until the mixture is combined well, and spread 1 tablespoon of this ginger-mayonnaise mixture on each piece of toast. Arrange the radishes, alfalfa sprouts, and shrimp on top of each canapé. Place on a serving dish, and garnish with watercress or cilantro. Stir the lemon juice into the remaining mayonnaise, and serve canapés with the mayonnaise drizzled over them.

Cheese Balls – LEBANON

In Lebanon, these cheese balls would be made of a salted feta-like goat cheese called *gibna arish.*
Here, an unripened chèvre log leavened with feta makes a very acceptable alternative.

INGREDIENTS

8-OUNCE LOG UNRIPENED CHÈVRE
    CHEESE
6 OUNCES FETA CHEESE
½ TEASPOON GROUND CUMIN
¼ TEASPOON CAYENNE PEPPER
3 TABLESPOONS FINELY CHOPPED MINT
    OR THYME LEAVES
4 TABLESPOONS OLIVE OIL

serves 12 to 15

METHOD

Combine the cheeses, cumin, and cayenne in a bowl, and mash together thoroughly. Take out small spoonfuls of cheese, and form into bite-sized balls. Roll the balls in the chopped herbs, and chill until firm. Before serving, mound the balls on a plate, and drizzle the olive oil over them.

Apricot and Cheese Mounds — LEBANON

INGREDIENTS

¾ CUP CREAM CHEESE

½ CUP SHELLED AND SKINNED
   HAZELNUTS

1 TEASPOON FRESHLY GROUND BLACK
   PEPPER

½ TEASPOON CAYENNE PEPPER

25 READY-TO-EAT DRIED APRICOTS

4 TABLESPOONS POPPY SEEDS

serves 12 to 15

The influence of the Ashkenazi Jews is evident in the use of poppy seeds in this recipe. For a more Arabic flavor, substitute toasted sesame seeds or pine nuts for the poppy seeds.

METHOD

Preheat the oven to 350°F. Work the cream cheese in a bowl until creamy. Spread the hazelnuts on a baking sheet, and cook for about 8 minutes, or until toasted. Remove, chop roughly, and stir into the cheese. Season with the pepper and cayenne, and combine thoroughly. Lay out the dried apricots, and divide the mixture between them. Form each into a smooth mound. Roll the tops of the mounds in the poppy seeds to coat, then chill for 2 to 3 hours, until firm.

Crab Roulade – AMERICA

INGREDIENTS

FOR THE ROULADE

2 TABLESPOONS BUTTER

4 TABLESPOONS ALL-PURPOSE FLOUR

¼ TEASPOON SALT

1 CUP HOT MILK

4 EGGS, SEPARATED

2 TABLESPOONS SNIPPED CHIVES

FOR THE CRAB SPREAD

⅓ CUP CREAM CHEESE

1–2 TABLESPOONS MILK

2 SCALLIONS, FINELY CHOPPED

1 TEASPOON LEMON JUICE

1 TEASPOON CAPERS, DRAINED AND
    CHOPPED

⅛ TEASPOON CAYENNE PEPPER

¾ CUP FRESH CRAB MEAT

serves 20 to 25

This elegant hors d'oeuvre is made by spreading a rich crab filling over very thin sponge, rolling it into a cylinder, then slicing it into pinwheels. It is not difficult to make, and can be assembled ahead of time. The roulade showcases the flavor of crab, so use fresh crab meat.

METHOD

Preheat the oven to 375°F. Line a 10 x 15-inch jelly roll pan or baking sheet with baking parchment. Butter the parchment. Melt the butter in a small saucepan. Whisk in the flour and salt, then the hot milk. Continue cooking and whisking until the mixture is thick and smooth. Remove from the heat. Add a tablespoon of the hot mixture to the egg yolks and whisk. Add several more spoonfuls, one at a time, then pour the yolk mixture into the pan with the remaining milk mixture. Add the chives. Whisk until smooth. In a medium bowl, beat the egg whites until soft peaks form. Gently fold into the hot mixture. Spread the mixture evenly over the buttered parchment. Bake at 375°F until the roulade is lightly browned, 15 to 20 minutes. Don't worry if it cracks or puffs up. Pierce any puffy spots with a knife tip. The roulade will "heal" itself as it cools. When the roulade is cool, cover it with a clean dish towel, and turn it upside down so it sits on the towel. Carefully peel off the parchment. Cut the roulade in half across its width. To make the crab spread, in a small bowl, thin the cream cheese with the milk until it has the consistency of soft butter. It must not be runny. Add the scallions, lemon juice, capers, and cayenne pepper, and mix well. Pick over the crab meat with your fingers to remove any bits of shell or cartilage. Stir the crab meat into the cream cheese mixture. Gently spread the crab mixture thinly across the surface of both rectangles, going to the very edge. Starting with the cut edge, roll each roulade into a tight cylinder, so you have two 7½-inch rolls. There should be enough crab spread at the end of the roulade, that the edge of the dough sticks to the cylinder. Note: The recipe may be prepared up to this point a day in advance. Don't slice the roulade more than a couple of hours in advance, or it may dry out. Slice the roulade into thin pinwheels of about ⅓ to ½ inch each. Arrange on a plate, and refrigerate until serving time.

Stuffed Bekkah Radishes – LEBANON

INGREDIENTS

1 POUND RADISHES

⅓ CUP CREAM CHEESE

1 TABLESPOON CHOPPED CAPERS

¾ CUP BOTTLED KALAMATA OLIVE PURÉE,
   DRAINED

1½ TABLESPOONS FINELY CHOPPED FLAT-
   LEAFED PARSLEY

FLAT-LEAFED PARSLEY SPRIGS,
   TO GARNISH

serves 16

Plump French-style radishes grown in the valleys are a popular hors-d'oeuvre in Beirut. But the method of presentation is unashamedly Middle-Eastern.

METHOD

Trim the radishes, so that they will stand on either end. Cut the radishes in half, and drop them into a bowl of ice water to crisp. One at a time, using a sharp knife or a melon-baller, hollow out a small hole in each half. Return to the ice water until all the radishes are done. Remove and drain upside down on paper towels.

In a bowl, beat together the cheese, capers, olive purée, and chopped parsley until thoroughly combined. Either pipe the filling into the halves, or carefully fill with a small spoon, and shape the filling with a fork. Garnish each radish with a parsley sprig.

Prosciutto Shrimp – ITALY

Prosciutto is Italian ham that has been cured in a spiced brine, then air-dried and aged for about a year. Because its flavor is so concentrated by this process, only a paper-thin slice is needed. In this simple but elegant appetizer, fruit and shrimp are wrapped in prosciutto and topped with Mango Salsa. If serving as a first course, allow three per person.

METHOD

Toss the shrimp with the lime juice. Let stand for 5 minutes, then drain off the juice if necessary. Pair each shrimp with a fig quarter or melon wedge. Cut large slices of prosciutto in half lengthwise. Wrap prosciutto around the fruit and shrimp. For the Mango Salsa, combine all the ingredients together. Top the shrimp with the salsa.

INGREDIENTS

12 MEDIUM TO LARGE SHRIMP, COOKED
   AND CLEANED

2 TABLESPOONS LIME JUICE

3 FRESH FIGS, QUARTERED, OR 12
   SMALL WEDGES OF HONEYDEW
   MELON

6 LARGE OR 12 SMALL SLICES OF
   PROSCIUTTO

FOR THE MANGO SALSA

2 MANGOES, PEELED, PITTED AND DICED

½ CUP CHOPPED RED ONION

⅔ CUP CHOPPED RED BELL PEPPER

2 FRESH JALAPEÑO CHILIES, SEEDED AND
   CHOPPED

3 TABLESPOONS LIME JUICE

serves 4

Island Shrimp Pocket Canapés – AMERICA

In this recipe the shrimp are marinated in a spicy vinaigrette, which gives them their punch. They can be marinated overnight, which makes this a perfect make-ahead dish for a party. All you need to do on the day is toast the pocket breads!

METHOD

In a saucepan, whisk together the vinegar, oil, sugar, Worcestershire sauce, Tabasco sauce, mustard, root ginger, and salt and pepper to taste. Bring the mixture to a boil, and simmer it, stirring occasionally, for 5 minutes. Add the shrimp and simmer, stirring occasionally, for 3 to 5 minutes, or until they are cooked through. Transfer the mixture to a heatproof bowl, and add the bell peppers, tossing the mixture well. Chill, covered, for at least 2 hours or overnight. Drain the mixture, discarding the liquid, and stir in the cilantro, red chili flakes if using, and salt and pepper to taste. Arrange the shrimp and several bell pepper strips on each pocket bread wedge, and garnish with cilantro sprigs.

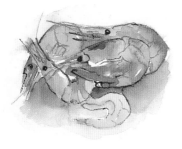

INGREDIENTS

¼ CUP CIDER VINEGAR

GENEROUS ¼ CUP VEGETABLE OIL

1½ TEASPOONS SUGAR

1 TEASPOON WORCESTERSHIRE SAUCE

DASH OF TABASCO SAUCE

½ TEASPOON DRY MUSTARD POWDER

1 TEASPOON PEELED AND MINCED
   GINGER ROOT

SALT AND FRESHLY GROUND
   BLACK PEPPER

1 CUP COOKED SHRIMP, SHELLED AND
   DEVEINED

¼ RED BELL PEPPER, THINLY SLICED

¼ YELLOW BELL PEPPER, THINLY SLICED

¼ GREEN BELL PEPPER, THINLY SLICED

1 TABLESPOON FINELY CHOPPED FRESH
   CILANTRO

DRIED HOT RED CHILI FLAKES
   (OPTIONAL)

4 LARGE, OR 8 SMALL, POCKET BREADS,
   CUT INTO ABOUT 12 WEDGES AND
   TOASTED LIGHTLY

CILANTRO LEAVES, TO GARNISH

serves 4 to 6

Marinated Fish Rolls – POLAND

INGREDIENTS

2½ CUPS WATER

1 BAY LEAF

1 ONION, THINLY SLICED

SALT AND FRESHLY GROUND
    BLACK PEPPER

2 TABLESPOONS VINEGAR

4 MACKEREL OR HERRINGS, CLEANED
    WITH HEADS OFF

1 SMALL CARROT

1 PICKLED CUCUMBER

1 PICKLED CUCUMBER, SLICED,
    TO GARNISH

DILL SPRIGS, TO GARNISH

serves 4

Use the freshest possible fish. If you are using mackerel, look for small, young specimens that tend to be fine-flaked and not over rich. The fish rolls may be served with boiled potatoes and beet salad, or accompanied by rye bread.

METHOD

Simmer the water, bay leaf, onion, and seasoning for 10 minutes with a close-fitting lid on the pan. Add the vinegar and cool. Bone the fish: lay each one flesh side down on a board, and press firmly down the middle of the bone. Turn the fish over, and the main bone should lift off easily, bringing with it most of the small bones at the side. Pick off all the remaining bones. Cut each fish in half lengthways to give eight fillets. Cut eight thin sticks from the carrot, and blanch them in boiling water for 1 minute. Drain and rinse under cold water. Cut eight thin sticks lengthways from the pickled cucumber. Place a stick of carrot and pickled cucumber at the wide end of each fish fillet and roll up to the tail, then secure with wooden toothpicks. Place in the prepared, cooled liquid. Heat very slowly until the liquid is steaming but not simmering. Cover and leave at this heat for 10 minutes. Remove from the heat, and let the fish cool completely in the liquid. The rolls should be cooked through by the time they have cooled. Lift the fish rolls from the cooking liquid when cool. Serve garnished with pickled cucumber and dill, whole or chopped.

Cream Cheese Curried Canapés – AMERICA

Here's an easy-to-make sandwich that is a creative garnisher's dream. You can top these canapés with all sorts of goodies, such as chopped chives, chopped walnuts, slivered toasted almonds, sliced scallions, watercress, raisins, toasted flaked coconut, a dollop of chutney, a chunk of fresh mango or papaya – you name it.

METHOD

Beat the cream cheese with an electric mixer until it is fluffy. Stir in the marmalade and curry powder. Cut two 2-inch rounds out of each bread slice with a biscuit cutter. Spread 1½ teaspoons of cream cheese mixture on each bread round. Garnish as desired.

INGREDIENTS

4 X 8-OUNCE PACKAGES CREAM CHEESE, SOFTENED

2 TABLESPOONS ORANGE MARMALADE

1 TEASPOON CURRY POWDER

8 THIN SLICES WHITE BREAD

serves 4 to 6

Golden Baskets – THAILAND

A classy opening dish to a meal, these crisp, deep-fried batter cases can also be presented as a delicate snack. The only significant problem is to find a suitable metal mold; a tiny ladle might do, but the dimensions should be no more than 2 inches across. The Thai molds are made from brass. You can make these cases in advance; sealed in a cooky barrel or jar, they will keep for a long time.

METHOD

Mix all the batter ingredients together well in a bowl. Heat the oil in a pan or wok to about 350°F. Dip the kratong molds in the oil to heat up, remove and pat lightly with paper towels. Then dip the outside of the molds into the batter and quickly into the hot oil again. Fry until light brown, about 5 to 8 minutes. Remove the cups from the molds, and place on paper towels to dry. Repeat to make between twenty to twenty five cups. Now make the filling. Put the oil in a hot wok or pan, add the onion and pork, and stir-fry for 2 minutes. Add the remaining ingredients, and fry until the vegetables are fairly soft, about 3 minutes. Take off the heat and let cool. Divide the filling between the batter cups. Garnish with cilantro leaves and small pieces of fresh red chili. Serve as an hors d'oeuvre or with cocktails.

INGREDIENTS

FOR THE BATTER

½ CUP RICE FLOUR

6 TABLESPOONS ALL-PURPOSE FLOUR

4 TABLESPOONS THIN COCONUT MILK

2 TABLESPOONS TAPIOCA FLOUR

1 EGG YOLK

¼ TEASPOON SUGAR

¼ TEASPOON SALT

¼ TEASPOON BAKING SODA

3¾ CUPS PEANUT OR CORN OIL FOR DEEP-FRYING

FOR THE FILLING

2 TABLESPOONS PEANUT OR CORN OIL

4 TABLESPOONS FINELY DICED ONION

6 OUNCES FINELY CHOPPED, COOKED PORK OR CHICKEN

CORN

2 TABLESPOONS FINELY CHOPPED, RAW POTATO

2 TABLESPOONS FINELY CHOPPED CARROT

2 TABLESPOONS SUGAR

¼ TEASPOON BLACK SOY SAUCE

½ TEASPOON SALT

½ TEASPOON GROUND WHITE PEPPER

CILANTRO LEAVES, TO GARNISH

1 SMALL FRESH RED CHILI, SLICED FINELY INTO CIRCLES, TO GARNISH

serves 4 to 6

Smoked Fish Mayonnaise and Garlic Toast – SPAIN

METHOD

Stew the bell peppers over a low heat in the oil, add black pepper and the tomato. Cover and stew for 20 minutes, or until soft. Cool. Skin and bone the fish, mix the mayonnaise into it, and blend in a food processor with black pepper. It should reach heavy cream consistency; add more garlic mayonnaise if necessary. Brush the bread on both sides with the garlic and 2 tablespoons olive oil. Bake in the oven until golden. Spoon a little of the pepper mixture over the bread toasties. Spoon some smoked fish mix onto the pepper and serve – Spanish club sandwich style!

INGREDIENTS

2 GREEN BELL PEPPERS, SEEDED AND CUT INTO THIN STRIPS

4 TABLESPOONS OLIVE OIL

PINCH OF FRESHLY GROUND BLACK PEPPER

1 TOMATO, PEELED AND CHOPPED

8 OUNCES SMOKED MACKEREL

8 OUNCES SMOKED COD (YOU COULD USE COOKED SALT COD)

½ CUP GARLIC MAYONNAISE

6 SLICES OF BREAD, CUT INTO TRIANGLES, OR 1 FRENCH STICK, CUT IN ROUNDS

1 TEASPOON CRUSHED GARLIC

2 TABLESPOONS OLIVE OIL

serves 4 to 6

Louisiana-style Cold Shrimp in Horseradish Sauce – AMERICA

These pungent, spicy shrimp are easy to make, and have the advantage of being prepared ahead. Serve as an appetizer, with lots of toothpicks and napkins on the side.

METHOD

In a bowl, combine all the ingredients, except the shrimp, and mix well. Add the shrimp making sure each piece is well coated. Refrigerate for at least 3 hours or as long as 24 hours.

INGREDIENTS

2 TABLESPOONS CIDER VINEGAR

2 TABLESPOONS LEMON JUICE

3 TABLESPOONS OLIVE OIL

2 GARLIC CLOVES, FINELY CHOPPED

3 TABLESPOONS CHOPPED SCALLIONS

2 TABLESPOONS FINELY CHOPPED FRESH PARSLEY

1 TEASPOON DRIED RED PEPPER FLAKES

1 TEASPOON CREOLE MUSTARD

2 TABLESPOONS DIJON MUSTARD

2 TABLESPOONS PREPARED HORSERADISH

½ TEASPOON CELERY SEED

1 PINT MEDIUM COOKED SHRIMP, SHELLED AND DEVEINED

serves 4 to 6

◀ **Smoked fish mayonnaise and garlic toast**

Stuffed Grape Leaves – LEBANON

Stuffed grape leaves are popular all over the eastern Mediterranean crescent, from Greece to Egypt. Unlike some of these nationalities, however, the Lebanese prefer their stuffing without meat and served cold.

INGREDIENTS

6-OUNCE PACKAGE GRAPE LEAVES
  (ABOUT 35)

4 TABLESPOONS OLIVE OIL

2 TABLESPOONS PINE NUTS

1 LARGE FINELY CHOPPED ONION

1 CUP LONG GRAIN RICE

SALT AND FRESHLY GROUND BLACK
  PEPPER

1 TABLESPOON RAISINS

1½ TEASPOONS FINELY CHOPPED MINT

½ TABLESPOON CINNAMON

JUICE OF 2 LEMONS

LEMON WEDGES, TO GARNISH

serves 15 to 25

METHOD

Remove the grape leaves from the package, separate them, place in a large container and pour boiling water over them. Let soak for 15 minutes, then drain. Return to the bowl, pour cold water on them, soak for 10 minutes longer, then drain thoroughly on paper towels. Heat 1 tablespoon of the olive oil in a large skillet. Add the pine nuts and sauté, stirring, for about 4 minutes, or until the nuts are golden. Remove the pine nuts with a slotted spoon and reserve. Add another 1 tablespoon of oil to the pan, and stir in the onions. Sauté until limp and lightly colored, about 5 to 6 minutes, then add the rice and salt to taste. Stir the rice until it is coated with the oil, then pour in ½ cup boiling water to cover. Reduce the heat, cover, and cook over medium heat for about 5 minutes. Take off the heat and let sit until the water has been absorbed, and the rice is tender – about 20 minutes. Stir in the raisins, pine nuts, chopped mint and cinnamon. Lay a grape leaf flat, and spoon 2 tablespoons

of the rice mixture near the stem end. Roll the leaf one turn over the mixture, then tuck in the sides of the leaf toward the center. Continue to roll the leaf like a cigar, until you reach the end. Squeeze the bundle to remove excess moisture. Repeat the process with the remaining leaves and stuffing. If there are any grape leaves left over, lay them on the bottom of a lightly oiled casserole. Arrange the stuffed leaves in a single layer on top. Pour over the lemon juice and just enough hot water to cover. Drizzle over the remaining 2 tablespoons olive oil. Weight the stuffed leaves down with a plate. Cover tightly and cook over high heat for about 4 minutes; then lower the heat, and simmer for about 40 minutes. Remove from the heat, uncover and let cool in the cooking liquid. When cold, remove the stuffed leaves with a slotted spoon, and arrange on a platter. Serve at room temperature or chilled, together with lemon wedges to squeeze over.

Rice Crackers with Pork and Coconut Sauce – THAILAND

INGREDIENTS

1¼ POUNDS COOKED RICE

3¾ CUPS PEANUT OR CORN OIL

1 TEASPOON CHOPPED CILANTRO ROOT

1 TEASPOON CHOPPED GARLIC

2 CUPS THIN COCONUT MILK

1 CUP CHOPPED, COOKED PORK

⅔ CUP CHOPPED, RAW SHELLED SMALL
  SHRIMP

1 TEASPOON CHOPPED FRESH CILANTRO

1 FRESH RED CHILI, CUT INTO STRIPS

1¼ CUPS FINELY CHOPPED UNSALTED
  PEANUTS

2 TABLESPOONS SLICED SHALLOTS

¼ TEASPOON GROUND WHITE PEPPER

½ TABLESPOON PALM SUGAR

1 TEASPOON SALT

serves 4 to 6

METHOD

Knead the rice slightly until it is sticky; then press it onto a slightly oiled non-stick baking pan in a layer ¼ inch thick. Place in a preheated oven at 375°F until very dry, 3 to 5 hours. Then, remove the rice from the pan, and break it into 2-inch pieces. Heat the oil in a wok or pan to a temperature of 350°F. Fry the rice crackers until a light tan color, 3 to 5 minutes. Remove them with a slotted spoon, and drain well on paper towels. To make the sauce, pound the cilantro

root and garlic together in a pestle and mortar. Heat the coconut milk in a pan, and add the cilantro and garlic mixture. Bring to a boil, add the pork, shrimp, and remaining ingredients, and continue to boil until the meat is cooked, about 7 to 10 minutes. Remove the pan from the heat, pour the sauce into a bowl and sprinkle with the cilantro leaf and chili. Serve the sauce with the rice crackers.

Pickled Shrimp – AMERICA

Pickled shrimp should be made at least 8 hours before you plan to serve them, but they're even better if you make them the night before. Set it out in a pretty dish, with toothpicks for serving.

INGREDIENTS

1 QUART MEDIUM OR LARGE SHRIMP

1 LEMON, HALVED

2 DRIED RED CHILIES

1 TABLESPOON WHOLE MUSTARD SEEDS

1 TEASPOON BLACK PEPPERCORNS

1 TABLESPOON WHOLE CORIANDER
    SEEDS

FOR THE MARINADE

1½ CUPS WHITE WINE VINEGAR

¾ CUP GOOD QUALITY OLIVE OIL

2 TABLESPOONS DIJON MUSTARD

1 ONION, THINLY SLICED

1 LEMON, SEEDED AND THINLY SLICED

1 TABLESPOON WHOLE MUSTARD SEEDS

1 TABLESPOON WHOLE CORIANDER
    SEEDS

1½ TEASPOONS DRIED RED CHILI FLAKES

3 GARLIC CLOVES, FINELY CHOPPED

½ TEASPOON SALT

serves 10

METHOD

Bring a large pan of water to a boil. Add the lemon, chilies, and spices. Boil for at least 20 minutes to develop the flavor. While the water is boiling, shell and devein the shrimp. Add the shrimp to the water, and cook until the shrimp turn an opaque white-pink and curl tightly, 2 to 3 minutes, depending on their size. Do not overcook, or the shrimp will be tough. Drain the shrimp, and plunge them into cold water to stop the cooking. Drain well. Put the shrimp in a glass or other non-reactive bowl. Pour the marinade over them, and turn the shrimp so all are coated. Refrigerate for at least 8 hours or up to 24 hours, stirring occasionally. To make the marinade, whisk together the oil, vinegar and mustard. Stir in the remaining ingredients and mix well.

Mushroom Cups – AMERICA

INGREDIENTS

FOR THE SHELLS

24 SLICES SOFT WHITE BREAD

¼ CUP MELTED BUTTER

¼ TEASPOON PAPRIKA

FOR THE FILLING

3 TABLESPOONS BUTTER

2 GARLIC CLOVES, FINELY CHOPPED

5 CUPS COARSELY CHOPPED
   MUSHROOMS

⅓ CUP CHOPPED SCALLIONS

1 TABLESPOON ALL-PURPOSE FLOUR

½ TEASPOON SALT

¼ TEASPOON BLACK PEPPER

⅛ TEASPOON CAYENNE PEPPER

2 TABLESPOONS SHERRY

⅓ CUP SOUR CREAM

serves 12

Crisp bread shells are filled with a sour cream and mushroom mixture for a hot hors d'oeuvre. This appetizer can be made up to 24 hours ahead, reheated before serving.

METHOD

Preheat the oven to 400°F. With a cooky cutter or glass, cut a 2½-inch round from each slice of bread. (Save the bread scraps to make bread crumbs.) Mix the melted butter and paprika. Lightly butter the cups of two mini-muffin pans. Gently press a round of bread into each cup. Using a pastry brush, lightly brush the inside of each bread cup with the remaining melted butter. You don't have to cover every spot or saturate the bread with butter. Bake at 400°F until the bread is crisp, 8 to 10 minutes. To

make the filling, preheat the oven to 350°F. Sauté the garlic, mushrooms, and scallions in the melted butter for 10 minutes. Sprinkle the flour, salt, pepper, and cayenne pepper over the mushrooms, stir well and cook for 1 minute. Add the sherry. Stir and cook until the sherry evaporates, about 1 minute. Remove from the heat, and stir in the sour cream. Divide the filling among the bread shells. Bake for 10 minutes if the filling is hot, 15 minutes if it has been made ahead and refrigerated.

Olives Beirut-style – LEBANON

Far more varieties and colors of olives are found in the Middle East than in other parts of the world. Round and torpedo-shaped; green, purple and black; pickled in myriad combinations of brine, vinegars and oils, they are a *meze* staple. These are lemon-zingy.

METHOD

In a bowl or jar with a cover, combine the olive oil, lemon juice, garlic, lemon peel and dill seed. Stir thoroughly to combine. Add the olives and agitate to mix well. Cover and chill for three days or up to one week.

INGREDIENTS

4 TABLESPOONS VIRGIN OLIVE OIL

2 TABLESPOONS LEMON JUICE

2 GARLIC CLOVES

1 TEASPOON GRATED LEMON RIND

½ TEASPOON DILL SEED

1 x 14-OUNCE CAN PITTED BLACK OR GREEN OLIVES, DRAINED

serves 10

Curried Chicken Salad in Puffs – AMERICA

Too many people are intimidated by cream puff shells. They are really not that daunting. Here, they're filled with chicken salad for delicious hors d'oeuvre or picnic finger food. Try other savory fillings, such as crab or ham salad. The puffs and salad can be made early in the day, then assembled about an hour before serving.

METHOD

Preheat the oven to 400°F. Cover two baking sheets with foil or baking parchment, then grease the parchment. Bring the milk, butter and salt to a boil in a medium saucepan. Add all the flour at once. Stir constantly until the mixture turns into a thick dough that pulls away from the sides of the pan. Remove from the heat. Add one egg at a time, beating the dough with a wooden spoon until each egg is fully incorporated before adding the next. Using a spoon or a piping bag, form the dough into walnut-sized balls. Place the balls on the baking sheets. Bake for 10 minutes at 400°F, then reduce the heat to 350°F, and bake until the puffs are golden brown, about 25 minutes. Cool away from any drafts. When the puffs are cool, slice off the tops with a sharp knife. Remove any soft center from inside. Fill with chicken salad and replace the tops. Keep refrigerated until serving time. Now to the salad. If the peaches are very juicy, set them in a colander to drain while you mix the other ingredients. Or go ahead and put them in the salad; you'll just have a juicier salad. Combine the chicken, peaches, grapes, almonds, scallions, and celery in a medium bowl. In a separate bowl, mix the mayonnaise, sour cream, curry powder, and salt. Add the dressing to the salad, and mix thoroughly. If the salad seems dry, add a little mayonnaise. To avoid soggy puffs, fill the puffs with the salad no more than 1 hour before serving time.

INGREDIENTS

FOR THE PUFFS

1 CUP MILK

5 TABLESPOONS BUTTER

PINCH OF SALT

1 CUP ALL-PURPOSE FLOUR

4 EGGS AT ROOM TEMPERATURE

FOR THE CURRIED CHICKEN SALAD

12 OUNCES COOKED CHICKEN, CUT INTO STRIPS

1 LARGE OR 2 SMALL PEACHES, PEELED AND CUBED

½ CUP SMALL SEEDLESS GRAPES

¼ CUP SLIVERED ALMONDS

2 TABLESPOONS CHOPPED SCALLIONS

¼ CUP CHOPPED CELERY

⅓ CUP MAYONNAISE

⅓ CUP SOUR CREAM

2 TEASPOONS CURRY POWDER

¼ TEASPOON SALT

serves 12 to 25

Hot

Bites

~

Samosas – INDIA

INGREDIENTS

FOR THE FILLING

3 TABLESPOONS OIL

¼ TEASPOON WHOLE CUMIN SEEDS

1 POUND POTATOES, DICED INTO
  ½-INCH CUBES

1 FRESH GREEN CHILI, FINELY CHOPPED

PINCH OF TURMERIC

½ TEASPOON SALT

⅔ CUP PEAS

1 TEASPOON GROUND ROASTED CUMIN

FOR THE DOUGH

2 CUPS ALL-PURPOSE FLOUR

1 TEASPOON SALT

3 TABLESPOONS OIL

APPROX ⅓ CUP HOT WATER

OIL FOR DEEP-FRYING

serves 12

METHOD

For the filling, heat the oil in a karai over medium high heat and add the cumin seeds. Let them sizzle for a few seconds. Add the potatoes and green chili, and fry for 2 to 3 minutes. Add the turmeric and salt, and, stirring occasionally, cook for 5 minutes. Add the peas and the ground roasted cumin. Stir to mix. Cover, lower the heat and cook 10 minutes longer until the potatoes are tender. Cool. For the dough, sift together the flour and salt. Rub in the oil. Add enough water to form a stiff dough. Knead for 10 minutes until smooth. Divide into twelve balls. Roll each ball into a round of about 6 inches across. Cut in half. Pick up one half, flatten it slightly and form a cone, sealing the overlapping edge with a little water. Fill the cone with 1½ teaspoons of the filling, and seal the top with a little water. In a similar way make all the samosas. Heat oil in a karai over medium heat. Put in as many samosas as you can into the hot oil, and fry until crisp and golden. Drain. Serve with a chutney.

Falafel – ISRAEL

INGREDIENTS

1 CUP DRIED GARBANZO BEANS,
   SOAKED AT LEAST 12 HOURS OR
   OVERNIGHT

1 SLICE DAY-OLD WHITE BREAD, CRUSTS
   REMOVED

1 MEDIUM ONION, QUARTERED

4 TO 5 GARLIC CLOVES, OR TO TASTE

2 TABLESPOONS CHOPPED FRESH
   CILANTRO OR PARSLEY

1 TABLESPOON GROUND CORIANDER

1 TABLESPOON GROUND CUMIN

2 TEASPOONS SALT

FRESHLY GROUND BLACK PEPPER

⅓ CUP BULGUR, RINSED AND DRAINED
   OR 3 TABLESPOONS ALL-PURPOSE
   FLOUR

1 TEASPOON BAKING POWDER

VEGETABLE OIL FOR DEEP-FRYING

These spicy, deep-fried garbanzo bean could almost be called the Israeli national dish, although they are also eaten all over the Middle East. They can be eaten on their own, as part of a *meze* or in a pocket bread with lettuce, tomato and cucumber.

METHOD

Drain and rinse the garbanzo beans. Sprinkle the bread with 1 tablespoon water, and let soak in, then squeeze out. Process the beans and bread to a semi-fine paste in a blender or food processor, you may need to work in batches. Transfer the mixture to a large bowl. Put onion quarters in the blender, and blend until finely chopped. Add the bean purée, and scrape blender well. Add garlic cloves to blender and blend until finely chopped. Add the cilantro or parsley to the garlic, and continue to blend until finely chopped. Add mixture to the beans and onions, and mix well. Add the ground coriander, cumin, and seasoning to taste. Stir in the bulgur or flour and baking powder. Using clean hands, mix the mixture very well. Using wet hands, shape about 1 tablespoon of mixture into a ball about the size of a walnut, rounding it between the palms of your hands; set the balls onto a baking sheet. Continue shaping until all mixture has been used. (Falafel can be prepared to this point several hours ahead.) Heat the oil to 350°F in a deep-fat fryer or deep saucepan. Add about one-quarter of the balls, sliding them carefully into the oil. Fry until a rich golden brown, 2 to 3 minutes. Remove with a slotted spoon to paper towels to drain. Repeat with remaining balls, one-quarter at a time. Serve warm in pocket breads with salad, pickled peppers, zhoug and tahini.

Vegetarian Spring Rolls – Vietnam

It is important to use ingredients that will not break through the delicate rice paper – that is why the ingredients must be ground, cut or grated finely. There must be no sharp edges. When you have practised with these ingredients, you could go on to substitute any of them with other vegetable ingredients.

INGREDIENTS

6 OUNCES BEAN THREAD VERMICELLI

4 DRIED CHINESE MUSHROOMS OR 6 BUTTON MUSHROOMS

1 PIECE LIGHT OR YELLOW WOOD EAR FUNGUS

1 PIECE BLACK WOOD EAR FUNGUS

1 SMALL CAN WATER CHESTNUTS, DRAINED AND CHOPPED

2 GARLIC CLOVES, CRUSHED

2 CARROTS, GRATED

2 ONIONS, GRATED

1 TABLESPOON NUOC MAM SAUCE OR 1 TABLESPOON LIGHT SOY SAUCE MIXED WITH ½ TABLESPOON ANCHOVY SAUCE

FRESHLY GROUND BLACK PEPPER

1 EGG, BEATEN

1 PACKAGE OF QUADRANT-SHAPED OR ROUND BANH TRANG RICE PAPER

VEGETABLE OIL FOR FRYING

1 ICEBERG OR ROUND LETTUCE

FRESH CILANTRO

MINT SPRIGS

½ CUCUMBER, PEELED AND CUT INTO MATCHSTICK SLICES

FOR THE DIPPING SAUCE

½ CUP NUOC MAM SAUCE OR ½ CUP LIGHT SOY SAUCE MIXED WITH ANCHOVY SAUCE

1 GARLIC CLOVE, FINELY CHOPPED

1 FRESH RED CHILI, FINELY CHOPPED

2 TEASPOONS LEMON OR LIME JUICE

1 TEASPOON WINE VINEGAR

1 TEASPOON SUGAR

½ CUP GRATED PEANUTS (OPTIONAL)

serves 6

METHOD

Make the dipping sauce first. Combine all the ingredients and stir thoroughly. Soak the vermicelli in boiled water, slightly cooled, until soft. Drain thoroughly. Use kitchen scissors to cut into shorter strands. Soak the Chinese mushrooms and the light and black wood ear fungus in boiled water, slightly cooled. When soft drain thoroughly, gently squeezing out any excess water. Cut finely. If using button mushrooms, wash, drain and chop finely. Place the vermicelli, water chestnuts, garlic, carrot, onion, light and black wood ear fungus, Nuoc Mam sauce, black pepper, and egg in a large mixing bowl. With your hands, mix and knead the mixture until it is stiff enough to be shaped. Pour some boiled water which has slightly cooled into a large bowl. Spread a clean dish towel on the surface you will be working on. Place the rice paper on the dish towel and repeat with another piece. The rice paper will turn soft and pliable. Place the second piece of rice paper on the first. The rounded edge of the quadrant should be at the bottom facing you and the second piece placed about 2 inches above but overlapping. Place a small portion of mixture where the pieces overlap at the bottom, at the rounded edge. Form the mixture into a sausage shape. Carefully roll the bottom edge over the mixture, tucking the edge under the mixture. Fold over the left and right sides to the middle, then roll the package away from you. Repeat these three steps until all the mixture has been used. Do not pack the rolls too tightly, otherwise they will burst when fried. When all the rolls are ready, heat the oil in a frying pan. Shallow fry, turning frequently until the mixture is cooked. Take care not to burn the rice paper. Place the rolls in the center of a lettuce leaf with some mint, cilantro and cucumber. Roll up and dip into the sauce while still hot.

Garlic Tapenade – France

INGREDIENTS

¼ CUP BLACK OLIVES

2–3 GARLIC CLOVES, COARSELY CHOPPED

3-OUNCE CAN ANCHOVIES

1 TABLESPOON CAPERS

½ CUP OLIVE OIL

A MEDIUM FRENCH LOAF, THINLY SLICED

serves 6

METHOD

Pit and coarsely chop the olives, and blend them with the garlic, anchovies and capers, adding the oil gradually. Toast the bread on one side. Spread the untoasted side thickly with the mixture, and cook under a hot broiler until the edges are well browned. Serve warm. This can also be served on fingers of crisp, buttered toast.

Fried Potato Cakes – INDIA

METHOD

Mix the mashed potatoes with the chilies, salt, cilantro leaves and onions. Form into small balls and flatten. Heat oil for shallow-frying until hot, and fry the potato cakes for a few minutes each side until golden. Serve with a chutney.

INGREDIENTS

1 POUND POTATOES, BOILED AND MASHED
1–2 FRESH GREEN CHILIES, CHOPPED
1 TABLESPOON CHOPPED FRESH CORIANDER
½ TEASPOON SALT
1 TABLESPOON CHOPPED ONION
OIL FOR FRYING

serves 12

Fried Polenta with Mushrooms – ITALY

METHOD

Melt one-third of the oil and the butter together over a medium heat. Add the mushrooms, garlic, and chilies, and fry together for 3 to 4 minutes over a high heat. Add the wine, tomatoes, parsley, and sage to the mixture. Reduce the heat to a simmer. As the mixture is cooking, slice the cold polenta into 1-inch slices. In a large, open pan, heat the remaining oil over a high heat. Fry each slice on both sides until a thin crust forms. Keep the slices hot if you do the frying in more than one batch. When all the polenta is fried, season the mushroom mixture, and spoon it generously over each slice. Eat it hot.

INGREDIENTS

2 TABLESPOONS OLIVE OIL
2 TABLESPOONS BUTTER
1½ POUNDS FIELD OR WOOD MUSHROOMS OR CEPS, COARSELY CHOPPED
2 GARLIC CLOVES, COARSELY CHOPPED
2 WHOLE SMALL CHILI PEPPERS, COARSELY CHOPPED
1 MEDIUM TOMATO, COARSELY DICED
4 TABLESPOONS RED WINE
1 TABLESPOON FINELY CHOPPED FRESH PARSLEY
1 TABLESPOON FINELY CHOPPED FRESH SAGE
SALT AND FRESHLY GROUND BLACK PEPPER TO TASTE

serves 6

Spicy Potato Patties – INDIA

METHOD

Peel and chop the potatoes, and boil them until they are tender. Meanwhile, mix the lemon juice, mint or mint sauce, and a pinch of salt into the onion. Set this mixture for filling the patties to one side. Break the potatoes, and mash them lightly so the mixture is still slightly lumpy. Add the coriander and cumin seeds, chili powder, green chilies, cilantro leaves and salt. Blend these herbs and spices well into the mashed potatoes. Divide the potato mixtures into eight equal portions. Dampen your hands a little, and roll each portion in your palm. Make a dent in the ball you've made, fill it with a tiny amount of the mint and onion filling, cover the filling, and flatten each ball gently to form a burger shape. Just before frying these patties, beat the egg, and season it lightly. Heat a large, nonstick skillet and grease it with half the oil. When the pan is fairly hot, dip each potato patty into the egg, and put it in the pan. Put the first four patties in the pan to sizzle for a minute or so, then turn them over, and cook the other side until they are crispy and golden brown. Cook the remaining four patties in the same way.

Stuffed Mushrooms – FRANCE

METHOD

Preheat the oven to 350°F. Wipe the mushrooms, and cut off the stems, as close as possible. Mash the butter and garlic together. Arrange the mushrooms, gill side up, on a greased baking sheet, and dot with the garlic and butter mixture. Cover with foil, and bake for 15 to 20 minutes, or until the mushrooms are just tender. Remove the foil, and top the mushrooms with the bread crumbs and parsley. Broil them at a high heat until the bread crumbs are browned.

Potato Streamers – ENGLAND

INGREDIENTS

2 LARGE POTATOES

2 GARLIC CLOVES, SLICED

½ CUP BUTTER

1 TABLESPOON GRATED PARMESAN
    CHEESE

SALT AND FRESHLY GROUND BLACK
    PEPPER

PINCH OF PAPRIKA

OIL FOR DEEP-FRYING

serves 4

METHOD

Preheat the oven to 425°F. Peel the potatoes, and cut into ¾-inch slices. Peel each slice round and round to form a long, thin ribbon. Soak the ribbons in ice water for at least an hour. Drain them and pat dry. Heat the garlic and butter slowly in a skillet until the garlic becomes transparent. Remove the garlic. Take the pan off the heat; dip each potato streamer into the hot, garlic butter, and lay them on a baking sheet. When all the streamers have been dipped, sprinkle the Parmesan over them, and season with salt, pepper, and a little paprika. Bake until crisp and well-browned which should take between 7 to 12 minutes. Serve warm. To deep-fry the dried streamers, drain on paper towels, and sprinkle with garlic salt. Serve immediately.

Green Banana Balls – INDIA

METHOD

Boil the banana until soft. Peel and cool. Mash the banana with the chili, cilantro leaves, salt, onion, and flour. Divide the mixture into eight small balls and flatten. Heat the oil, and deep-fry the koftas, turning once, until crisp and golden.

INGREDIENTS

1 GREEN BANANA, CUT IN HALF

1 GREEN CHILI, CHOPPED

½ TABLESPOON CHOPPED FRESH
    CILANTRO

½ TEASPOON SALT

1 TABLESPOON ALL-PURPOSE FLOUR

OIL FOR DEEP-FRYING

serves 8

Nachos – MEXICO

METHOD

Fry the onion or scallions with the chilies in a little of the oil until softened and beginning to brown. Drain and reserve. Add the oil to the pan, and fry the tortillas on both sides until golden. Drain each on paper towels, and keep warm while you fry the rest. Arrange the fried tortillas on a baking sheet, sprinkle with the onion and chili mixture, and top with grated cheese. Broil under a high heat until the cheese melts. Stack the Nachos, quarter them and serve.

INGREDIENTS

1 SMALL ONION OR 3 SCALLIONS, FINELY CHOPPED

2 FRESH GREEN CHILIES, SEEDED AND FINELY CHOPPED

3 TABLESPOONS OIL

8 BOUGHT CORN TORTILLAS

¼ CUP SHREDDED OR GRATED, SHARP CHEDDAR CHEESE

serves 32

Fried Garlic Haloumi – GREECE

METHOD

Cut the cheese into 1-inch cubes, and pack them into a shallow soufflé dish in a single layer. Sprinkle over the crushed garlic and herbs, and pour over the oil to cover the cheese cubes. Cover the dish with a plate, and leave in a cool place for at least 12 hours so that the flavors of the garlic and herbs permeate the cheese. To cook the haloumi, drain off the garlic oil, and fry the cheese in a few tablespoons of it until golden all over – about 6 minutes. Serve immediately with toothpicks.

INGREDIENTS

8 OUNCES HALOUMI CHEESE, AVAILABLE FROM MOST GREEK DELICATESSENS

3–4 GARLIC CLOVES, CRUSHED

1 TABLESPOON FRESH MIXED HERBS, CHOPPED

1¼ CUPS OLIVE OIL

serves 16

Garlic Cheesecake Tart – FRANCE

INGREDIENTS

PLAIN PASTRY DOUGH FOR 8-INCH TART
SHELL

1 GARLIC HEAD (ABOUT 12 CLOVES)

A HANDFUL OF PARSLEY

A HANDFUL OF WATERCRESS OR SPINACH

¾ CUP CREAM CHEESE

½ CUP LIGHT CREAM

3 EGGS, BEATEN

SALT AND FRESHLY GROUND
BLACK PEPPER

serves 6

METHOD

Preheat the oven to 425°F. Line an 8-inch quiche dish with the dough, and cover with foil. Fill with baking beans, and bake for 10 to 15 minutes until firm. Remove the baking beans and foil and let the pastry shell cool. Simmer the unpeeled garlic cloves for 25 minutes until soft. Drain and, when cool, mash to a paste. Cook the parsley and watercress or spinach in boiling water for 7 to 10 minutes until tender. Drain and refresh under cold water. Squeeze out the excess liquid, and chop finely. Mix with the garlic paste, seasoning with a little salt and pepper to taste. Spread the mixture over the bottom of the pastry shell. Mash the cream cheese with the cream and a little salt and pepper until smooth. Add the beaten eggs. Pour over the garlic paste, and bake at 350°F for about 25 minutes until just set. Serve warm.

Cheese Filo Triangles – GREECE

A classic Greek *meze* dish. Why not double the quantity and freeze half the triangles before baking – then you'll have something to fall back on when unexpected guests drop by.

METHOD

Preheat the oven to 400°F. Place the feta and cottage cheese in a medium-sized bowl, and mix well. Beat in the eggs, parsley, mint, and seasoning. To make the triangles, lay the filo pastry dough out on a work surface, and cover with a slightly damp cloth. Separate the first sheet of pastry, and lay it on the work surface, keeping the remaining sheets covered to prevent them drying out. Divide into three equal strips, and brush each strip lightly with the melted butter. Place 2 teaspoons of the cheese mixture toward the bottom right corner of the pastry strip. Fold that corner diagonally over to the top left corner, to make a small triangle. Then take the bottom left corner and fold it diagonally over to the top right hand corner, and so on, alternately folding the bottom corners in a diagonal pattern to finish up with a firm, neat triangle. Repeat the process with the other strips, and then continue with another sheet of pastry in the same way. You may need more than one buttered baking sheet. Bake the triangles for 15 to 20 minutes, or until lightly golden and crisp. Transfer the triangles to a wire rack and serve warm, or let cool.

INGREDIENTS

8 OUNCES FETA CHEESE

6 OUNCES COTTAGE CHEESE

2 EGGS, BEATEN

2 TABLESPOONS CHOPPED FRESH PARSLEY

1 TABLESPOON CHOPPED FRESH MINT

SALT AND FRESHLY GROUND BLACK PEPPER

8 OUNCES FILO PASTRY DOUGH, THAWED IF FROZEN

1 CUP MELTED BUTTER

serves 8 to 10

Shrimp with Sesame Seeds on Toast – THAILAND

INGREDIENTS

4 TABLESPOONS WHITE SESAME SEEDS

½ TABLESPOON DRIED SHRIMP
   (OPTIONAL)

¾ CUP FINELY CHOPPED SHELLED SHRIMP

2 GARLIC CLOVES, CRUSHED AND
   CHOPPED

½ TEASPOON GRATED FRESH GINGER
   ROOT

1 SMALL ONION, GRATED

1 SMALL EGG, BEATEN

SALT AND FRESHLY GROUND BLACK
   PEPPER

CORNSTARCH FOR DUSTING

1 THIN FRENCH STICK OR 8 SLICES
   BREAD, CRUSTS CUT OFF

VEGETABLE OIL FOR DEEP-FRYING

serves 4

METHOD

Toast the sesame seeds in a dry pan until they begin to brown, shaking frequently to prevent them from burning. If using dried shrimp, soak in warm water until soft. Drain thoroughly and squeeze out excess water. Chop them finely. Combine the dried and fresh shrimp, garlic, ginger, grated onion, egg, salt and black pepper, and knead together with your hands. The mixture should be stiff but not too stiff to spread. If it is too runny, dust with cornstarch. Cut the French bread into ½-inch slices, or cut the slices of bread into triangles or shape using cookie cutters. Press the sesame seeds firmly into the shrimp mixture, using the back of a wooden spoon so that the shrimp mixture is also pressed firmly on to the bread. Refrigerate for 2 hours or longer if possible. Heat just enough oil to deep-fry the rounds, shrimp side down, for 1 minute. Using a fish slice, turn carefully and fry the other side for a minute longer. Drain on paper towels,and serve hot.

Fish Kofta – INDIA

METHOD

Mash or process together all the ingredients except the eggs, bread crumbs and oil. Form into small balls, roll in the beaten egg and then in the bread crumbs, and deep or shallow-fry until golden. Drain on paper towels, and serve hot, with toothpicks and perhaps a choice of dips.

INGREDIENTS

12 OUNCES COOKED FIRM WHITE FISH

1 SMALL ONION, GRATED

1 TEASPOON GROUND CORIANDER

½ TEASPOON GROUND TURMERIC

½ TEASPOON GROUND CUMIN

½ TEASPOON CHILI POWDER

PINCH OF GROUND GINGER

1 TABLESPOON LIME JUICE

PINCH OF SALT

2 EGGS, LIGHTLY BEATEN

BREAD CRUMBS

OIL FOR SHALLOW OR DEEP-FRYING

serves 4 to 6

Cajun Popcorn – AMERICA

METHOD

Combine all the dry ingredients. Whisk in the eggs, butter and beer until smooth. Refrigerate for at least 3 hours to give the gluten in the flour a chance to expand. Whisk again before using. In a deep frying pan or wok heat 1½ inches of oil to 350°F. Pat the shrimp dry, then dip in the batter. Drop some of the shrimp in the oil, but don't crowd, and fry until golden brown, turning once, about 2 minutes in total. Drain well on paper towels, and keep warm while frying the remaining shrimp. Be sure the oil returns to 350°F before frying the next batch. Continue until all the shrimp are fried.

INGREDIENTS

¼ CUP CORNSTARCH

¼ CUP ALL-PURPOSE FLOUR

2 TABLESPOONS CORNMEAL

1 TEASPOON SALT

½ TEASPOON ONION POWDER

½ TEASPOON GARLIC POWDER

¼ TEASPOON CAYENNE PEPPER

LARGE PINCH OF FRESHLY GROUND
   BLACK PEPPER

2 EGGS, LIGHTLY BEATEN

1 TABLESPOON MELTED BUTTER

4 TABLESPOONS WARM BEER

1 QUART SMALL SHRIMP, SHELLED AND
   DEVEINED, OR CRAYFISH TAILS,
   SHELLED

VEGETABLE OIL FOR FRYING

serves 6 to 8

Stuffed Mussels – ITALY

INGREDIENTS

48 LARGE MUSSELS

DASH OF WHITE WINE

1 CUP UNSALTED BUTTER

10 GARLIC CLOVES, CRUSHED

2 CUPS FRESH BREAD CRUMBS

LEMON WEDGES, TO GARNISH

serves 24

METHOD

Debeard and scrub the mussels. Throw away any mussels that remain open when tapped. Steam open the mussels in a little white wine and water. Drain and take off the top shell. Soften the butter a little with your hands. Add the crushed garlic cloves, and work the bread crumbs into the garlic butter. Put a knob of the stuffing on each mussel, and place under a hot broiler. Serve very hot with lemon wedges and crusty French bread.

Conch Scotch Bonnet Fritters with Two Cool Dips – AMERICA

INGREDIENTS

1 PINT CONCH, CLAMS OR SQUID

3 CELERY STALKS, FINELY CHOPPED

1 ONION, FINELY CHOPPED

½ CUP BUTTER

1 TEASPOON MINCED FRESH CHILI

PINCH OF THYME

PINCH OF BASIL

PINCH OF OREGANO

PINCH OF SALT

PINCH OF FRESHLY GROUND BLACK
   PEPPER

¼ TEASPOON BAKING POWDER

4 EGGS

1½ CUPS ALL-PURPOSE FLOUR

SPLASH OF MILK

VEGETABLE OIL FOR DEEP-FRYING

FOR THE LIME DIP

1¼ CUPS SOUR CREAM

⅓ CUP MAYONNAISE

JUICE OF 2 LIMES

FOR THE AVOCADO-CRESS DIP

1 SMALL RIPE AVOCADO, PEELED AND
   PITTED

½ TABLESPOON MILK

½ TABLESPOON LEMON JUICE

¾ TEASPOON SALT

½ CUP WATERCRESS, TOUGH STEMS
   REMOVED

serves 4 to 6

METHOD

Put the conch, clams or squid through a blender or food processor. Fry the celery and onion in the butter for about 3 minutes. Add the chili, herbs, salt and pepper, and stir to blend thoroughly. Place the mixture in a large bowl together with the conch, baking powder, eggs, flour and milk. Mix well to a thick yet runny consistency, and chill. While the fritter batter is chilling, prepare the dips by mixing the ingredients in a blender or food processor at medium speed. Place the dips in the refrigerator to chill, about 30 minutes. When the fritter batter is chilled, heat the oil to 350°F for frying. Using a large oval spoon, form 1-inch thick dumplings, and drop them straight into the hot oil. Cook for about 4 to 6 minutes. Drain them on paper towels, and serve with the dips.

Malanga Pancakes with Caviar – AMERICA

This is a Nuevo Cubano version of Beauty and the Beast. The "Beauty" is, of course, the caviar that festoons these pancakes. The "Beast" is the malanga, a rather unattractive tuber before it's peeled. Serve with Vodka Dip (page 28).

METHOD

If using white potatoes rather than malanga, add 1 teaspoon ground walnuts to the egg mixture. If using white potatoes instead of boniato, add ¼ teaspoon allspice to the egg mixture. Squeeze the grated tubers in cheesecloth to remove excess water. Beat the egg in a bowl, then stir in the cilantro, garlic, lime juice, and salt. Stir in the grated tubers. Let stand for 20 minutes at room temperature to congeal. Heat the butter and oil to a medium heat in a large skillet. Stir in the batter, and divide into four small bowls or pitchers. In succession, pour half of the contents from each until you have made eight fairly uniform, 4-inch pancakes. Fry until golden brown for about 5 minutes, turning once. Place the pancakes on a warm platter, electric warming broiler or warming tray, and top each one with a thin layer of caviar, about 1 tablespoon per pancake. Serve immediately.

INGREDIENTS

- 4 OUNCES MALANGA OR WHITE POTATOES, PEELED AND GRATED ON LARGE HOLES OF GRATER
- 4 OUNCES BONIATO OR WHITE POTATOES, PEELED AND GRATED ON LARGE HOLES OF GRATER
- 1 EGG
- 1½ TABLESPOONS FINELY CHOPPED FRESH CILANTRO
- 1 GARLIC CLOVE, CRUSHED
- ½ TEASPOON LIME JUICE
- ½ TEASPOON SALT
- 1 TABLESPOON BUTTER
- 1 TABLESPOON VEGETABLE OIL
- 8 TABLESPOONS STURGEON CAVIAR

serves 4

Spinach Packages – LEBANON

These Levantine stuffed pastries were the prototypes of the Cornish pasties and meat pies which developed in Britain after the Crusades.

INGREDIENTS

FOR THE FILLING

2 POUNDS FRESH LEAF SPINACH,
    DRAINED AND CHOPPED

3 TABLESPOONS OLIVE OIL

1 ONION, GRATED

SEEDS OF 1 POMEGRANATE

1 CUP CRUSHED WALNUTS

1 TABLESPOON SUMAC (OPTIONAL)

JUICE OF 1½ LEMONS

SALT AND FRESHLY GROUND BLACK
    PEPPER

FOR THE DOUGH

LUKEWARM WATER

1 CAKE COMPRESSED YEAST OR ½
    TEASPOON DRY YEAST

2 CUPS ALL-PURPOSE FLOUR

1 TEASPOON SALT

1½–2 TABLESPOONS OLIVE OIL

OLIVE OIL, TO COAT

serves 12

METHOD

Squeeze as much moisture as possible from the spinach. Heat the oil in a skillet, and stir in the grated onion. Cook for 2 minutes, then add the spinach, and stir until it is thoroughly wilted. Add the pomegranate seeds, walnuts, sumac if using, and the lemon juice. Combine well, then take off the heat and set aside. Now make the dough. In a bowl, stir together half the water and yeast. Let rest for 15 minutes, or until mixture begins to foam. In another bowl, sift together the flour and salt. Make a well in the middle and pour in the oil, then the yeast mixture. Using your hands, pull the flour into the liquid, and begin to work into a dough. Add the remaining lukewarm water gradually. When all the dough sticks together and all the water has been added, knead the dough on a lightly floured surface for about 15 minutes. Pat the dough into a ball and then place the oil in a bowl. Turn the ball in the oil to coat, remove and cover with a damp cloth. Leave for about 2½ hours until it has doubled in size. Break off the dough into twenty-five pieces, and form into balls. On a floured board, roll the balls into small rounds as thin as possible. Divide the filling among the rounds. Place the filling in the center of each round, and bring up the sides to form three-sided packages. Pinch the top edges together. Preheat the oven to 375°F. Place the pastries on oiled baking sheets, and bake for 5 minutes. Then lower the heat to 350°F and continue baking for 15 to 20 minutes longer. Remove from the oven, and let them cool slightly before serving warm.

Deep-fried Fish Cakes – THAILAND

INGREDIENTS

10 OUNCES WHITE FISH

⅔ CUP COCONUT MILK OR COWS' MILK

1¼ CUPS BOILED AND MASHED SWEET
    POTATOES

2 TOMATOES, PEELED AND CHOPPED

2 TABLESPOONS CHOPPED FRESH
    CILANTRO

2 TABLESPOONS NUOC MAM SAUCE OR
    2 TABLESPOONS LIGHT SOY SAUCE
    MIXED WITH 1 TEASPOON ANCHOVY
    SAUCE

2 EGGS, LIGHTLY BEATEN

RICE FLOUR OR ALL-PURPOSE FLOUR

VEGETABLE OIL FOR DEEP-FRYING

LETTUCE LEAVES, TO GARNISH

SPRIGS OF MINT, TO GARNISH

serves 4

METHOD

Cover the fish with the coconut milk. (If there is not sufficient add a little water or cows' milk.) Bring the milk to a boil, and simmer for 10 minutes or until the fish is tender. Remove any skin or bones, and flake the fish. Place the fish, potato, tomatoes and cilantro in a bowl, and mix well. Combine the Nuoc Mam sauce and egg. Add half this mixture slowly to the fish mixture so that it retains its shape. Add some flour if the mixture is too runny. Shape the mixture into small balls. Dip each ball into the remaining egg and Nuoc Mam sauce mixture, and roll in the rice flour. Heat the oil until it is smoking, and deep-fry until the balls are golden brown. Serve hot, garnished with the lettuce and sprigs of mint.

Deep-fried fish cakes ▶

Jumbo Shrimp in Garlic – Spain

INGREDIENTS

3 TABLESPOONS OLIVE OIL

12 JUMBO SHRIMP, FRESH IF AVAILABLE;
    IF NOT, COOK FROM FROZEN

2 TEASPOONS CRUSHED GARLIC

2 TEASPOONS PAPRIKA

2 TABLESPOONS MEDIUM SHERRY

LEMON WEDGES, TO SERVE

serves 12

METHOD

Heat the oil in a pan. For frozen shrimp, lower heat. Add the shrimp to the oil, cover and cook for 6 minutes, until soft and heated through. For fresh shrimp, add to the oil until sizzling. Add the remaining ingredients, and bring to a boil. Taste for seasoning. Serve with lemon wedges.

Onion Bhajis – INDIA

INGREDIENTS

2 TABLESPOONS OIL

½ TEASPOON GROUND MUSTARD SEED

1 TEASPOON FENUGREEK SEED

1 TEASPOON GROUND TURMERIC

1 MEDIUM ONION, FINELY CHOPPED

PINCH OF CHILI POWDER (OPTIONAL)

½ TEASPOON SALT

1 EGG

1 CUP GARBANZO BEAN FLOUR

OIL FOR FRYING

serves 5 to 10

METHOD

Heat the oil, and fry the spices for a minute. Add the onion, and stir until well coated. Turn down the heat, cover, and cook until the onion is tender but not mushy. Let cool. Add the salt, egg, and garbanzo bean flour, and stir well. Fry generous half-tablespoonfuls of the mixture in ½ inch of hot oil, turning them almost immediately. As soon as they are puffy and brown, remove them with a slotted spoon and drain on paper towels. Serve warm. Onion Bhajis can be kept warm in a medium oven for 20 minutes or so before serving, but they cannot be made ahead and reheated.

Jumbo shrimp in garlic ▶

Blinis with Smoked Salmon and Sour Cream – RUSSIAN FEDERATION

INGREDIENTS

¼ CUP LUKEWARM WATER

1½ TEASPOONS DRY YEAST

½ CUP ALL-PURPOSE FLOUR

¾ CUP BUCKWHEAT FLOUR

½ TEASPOON SALT

1 CUP MILK

2 EGGS, SEPARATED

¼ CUP BUTTER OR MARGARINE

4 SCALLIONS, THINLY SLICED ON THE
   DIAGONAL

½ CUP SOUR CREAM

SNIPPED FRESH CHIVES, TO GARNISH

2 TABLESPOONS SOUR CREAM

4 OUNCES SMOKED SALMON OR LOX,
   THINLY SLICED

serves 6

Blinis are Russian pancakes made with buckwheat flour. They have a nutty flavor which is enhanced by smoked salmon or lox and sour cream. A less extravagant presentation can be offered with chopped radishes and cucumber, scallions and capers. Blinis make a wonderful brunch, or light lunch dish.

METHOD

Pour the lukewarm water into a small bowl, and sprinkle the yeast over. Let stand until the yeast becomes foamy and bubbly, about 5 minutes. Sift the flours, and salt into a large bowl, and make a well in center. Heat ¾ cup of the milk to lukewarm, and add it to the yeast mixture, stirring with a wire whisk and drawing in the flour little by little to form a smooth batter. Cover the bowl with a clean dish towel, and leave in a warm place until the batter becomes light and bubbly, 3 hours. Beat the remaining ¼ cup milk into the batter; beat the egg yolks and stir into the batter with half the butter, melted, and sour cream. In another bowl, with a hand-held mixer at medium speed, beat egg whites until stiff peaks form (do not overbeat). Fold the egg whites into the blini batter until just blended. (Do not overblend; a few white lumps will cook out.) Melt the remaining butter in a large skillet or on a griddle, over medium-high heat. Using a small ladle, pour the batter into the pan or griddle to form small pancakes. Cook until undersides are lightly browned, about 2 minutes. Turn the blinis over, and cook 1 to 2 minutes longer. Continue until all the batter is used, adding more butter if necessary. (Keep blinis warm in a 300°F oven if necessary.) Arrange the blinis on individual plates or on a large serving dish. Divide the smoked salmon or lox slices equally onto the blinis. Top each blini with a few sliced scallions and a spoonful of sour cream. Sprinkle with chives, and serve warm.

Sausage Balls – AMERICA

Sausage balls are easy to make, and you can vary them by using different types of sausage. Serve them with toothpicks and a bowl of good mustard for dipping.

INGREDIENTS

12 OUNCES SPICY PORK SAUSAGE

1 CUP GRATED CHEDDAR CHEESE

1 CUP ALL-PURPOSE FLOUR

2 TEASPOONS BAKING POWDER

⅓ CUP CHOPPED RED ONION

3 TABLESPOONS MILK

serves 15

METHOD

Preheat oven to 350°F. Crumble the sausage into a bowl. Add the remaining ingredients and knead them together. Shape the mixture into balls. You can make them to this point, and refrigerate them until shortly before serving time. Place the sausage balls in a shallow baking dish, and bake them for 15 to 20 minutes, or until browned. Drain briefly on paper towels, and serve while hot.

Bacon-wrapped Shrimp with Sour Cream – SPAIN

INGREDIENTS

12 JUMBO SHRIMP, SHELLED, LEAVING
   ON THE HEAD AND TAIL TIP (DEFROST
   OVERNIGHT IF USING FROZEN)

1 CUP GRATED FRESH MOZZARELLA
   CHEESE

1 TEASPOON FRESHLY GROUND BLACK
   PEPPER

12 SLICES GOOD BACON, TRIMMED OF
   THE RIND AND EXCESS FAT

DASH OF OLIVE OIL

FOR THE SAUCE/DIP

1 CUP SOUR CREAM

½ TEASPOON EACH SALT AND FRESHLY
   GROUND BLACK PEPPER

JUICE OF ½ LEMON

serves 6 to 12

METHOD

Make a slit lengthwise along the back of the shrimp, but do not cut through. Fill the slit with the cheese, mixed with the black pepper. Wrap each prawn in one slice of bacon, starting at the head, which should peep out, and slightly spiral the bacon to the tail. Paint with olive oil, and either broil or bake in a hot oven, 450°F, for 7 to 10 minutes. Meanwhile, prepare the dip. Mix all the ingredients together for the sauce, and serve with the hot shrimp.

Sausage balls ▶

Fried Chicken Balls – GREECE

The chicken mixture in this recipe could be formed into sausage shapes around skewers, and broiled or barbecued to be served as Chicken Koftas.

INGREDIENTS

3 CHICKEN BREASTS, SKINNED, BONELESS
   AND FINELY GROUND
1 CUP FRESH WHITE BREAD CRUMBS
½ CUP GROUND PINE NUTS
3 TABLESPOONS FINELY CHOPPED FRESH
   PARSLEY
½ TEASPOON GROUND TURMERIC
1 EGG, BEATEN
SALT AND FRESHLY GROUND
   BLACK PEPPER
FLOUR, FOR DREDGING
OLIVE OIL, FOR SHALLOW-FRYING
JUICE OF 1 LEMON, TO SERVE

serves 6 to 8

METHOD

Place the chicken in a mixing bowl, and add the bread crumbs, pine nuts, parsley, and turmeric. Mix well to combine. Add the beaten egg to the chicken mixture and season. With slightly damp hands, shape the chicken mixture into balls the size of walnuts, and place on a baking sheet lined with baking parchment. Sprinkle the balls lightly with flour. Heat the oil in a deep nonstick skillet and fry the chicken balls, a few at a time, for about 5 to 8 minutes or until crisp and cooked through, turning them to make sure they cook evenly. Transfer the cooked chicken balls to an ovenproof dish, and place in a low oven to keep warm while the remaining batches are cooked. Serve warm or cold, sprinkled with lemon juice.

Stuffed Chicken Wings – VIETNAM

INGREDIENTS
8 CHICKEN WINGS

FOR THE STUFFING
4 OUNCES BEAN THREAD VERMICELLI
3 PIECES DARK WOOD EAR FUNGUS
2½ CUPS GROUND PORK
1 SMALL ONION, FINELY GRATED
1 SMALL CARROT, FINELY GRATED
1 EGG, BEATEN
1 TABLESPOON NUOC MAM SAUCE OR
   LIGHT SOY SAUCE
SALT AND FRESHLY GROUND
   BLACK PEPPER

serves 4

METHOD

Bone the chicken wings by cutting around the bone with a sharp knife. Holding the wing tip, gently ease the bone away to leave the skin and a thin layer of chicken. Soak the vermicelli in warm water for 10 minutes, then drain thoroughly and cut into short strands. Soak the wood ear fungus in warm water for 10 minutes, then squeeze dry and chop into thin slices. Mix all the stuffing ingredients together. The mixture should be firm. Mold the stuffing into a ball, and insert it into the bag of flesh and skin of the chicken wings. Preheat the oven to 400°F. Steam the stuffed wings for 10 to 15 minutes. (If you want to make a large quantity, multiply the measures accordingly and freeze after the steaming stage.) After steaming, place in a lightly oiled roasting pan, and roast in the oven for 30 minutes. Serve on a bed of lettuce as an appetizer or with rice and a beef stir-fry dish.

New Orleans-style Chicken Skewers — AMERICA

Simple to make, these chicken skewers are marinated, then grilled on the barbecue. They can be served hot or cold, and are excellent finger foods for picnics and barbecues.

METHOD

Cut the chicken into four to five strips each. Combine the remaining ingredients to make the marinade. Put the chicken in a shallow glass or other nonreactive dish. Pour the marinade over the chicken, and turn it to be sure all pieces are coated. Marinate the chicken in the refrigerator for at least 5 hours. About 40 minutes before serving time, start a fire in the barbecue. If you are using wooden skewers, soak them in water for 30 minutes to avoid burning them. Thread the chicken onto the skewers so they form an S-curve. Do not crowd the chicken, as it will not cook evenly. If the skewers are long, you may put two strips of chicken on each. When the flames have died and the coals are glowing, place the skewers on the grid over the coals. Turn the skewers at least once so both sides are cooked. Cooking time will be 10 to 15 minutes.

INGREDIENTS

4 BONELESS CHICKEN BREASTS
½ CUP OLIVE OIL
1 TABLESPOON LIME JUICE
2 TABLESPOONS RED WINE VINEGAR
2 GARLIC CLOVES, FINELY CHOPPED
¼ TEASPOON CAYENNE PEPPER
¼ TEASPOON BLACK PEPPER
1 TABLESPOON CHOPPED FRESH BASIL, OR 1 TEASPOON DRIED
1 TABLESPOON CHOPPED FRESH OREGANO, OR 1 TEASPOON DRIED

serves 4

Crispy Meat-filled Ovals – GREECE

The crispy coating of the bulgur wheat surrounds a surprise filling of delicately flavored meat. Another Greek specialty, hard to resist.

INGREDIENTS

3 CUPS BULGUR WHEAT

1½ CUPS BOILING WATER

SALT AND FRESHLY GROUND
   BLACK PEPPER

2 TEASPOONS GROUND CINNAMON

1 TABLESPOON VEGETABLE OIL, PLUS
   EXTRA FOR DEEP-FRYING

1½ CUPS LEAN GROUND PORK

4 SCALLIONS, FINELY CHOPPED

2 TABLESPOONS CHOPPED FRESH
   PARSLEY

OIL FOR DEEP-FRYING

serves 8 to 10

METHOD

Place the bulgur wheat in a medium-sized bowl, and pour the boiling water over it. Season and stir in 1 teaspoon ground cinnamon. Set aside to cool, stirring occasionally. Meanwhile, to make the filling; heat 1 tablespoon oil in a skillet, and add the pork and onions. Sauté for about 10 to 15 minutes, or until the meat is no longer pink and is cooked through. Stir in the parsley, and add the remaining ground cinnamon. Season to taste, and set aside to cool. To shape the ovals, using slightly damp hands, take a small handful of the bulgur mixture, and form it into a ball. Using your forefinger and a teaspoon, make a hollow in the center of the ball, and fill it with the pork filling. Pinch the ends of the ball to make an oval, and set aside. Continue with the remaining mixture. Heat the oil in a deep-fat fryer, and cook the ovals in batches for 3 to 5 minutes, or until crisp, golden and heated through. Drain the cooked ovals on paper towels, and keep warm in a low oven while the other batches cook. Serve warm.

North-eastern Sausages – THAILAND

INGREDIENTS

1½ CUPS GROUND PORK

⅓ CUP COOKED RICE

2 TABLESPOONS LIME JUICE

1 TEASPOON CHOPPED GARLIC

1 TEASPOON GROUND WHITE PEPPER

½ TEASPOON SALT

¼ TEASPOON SUGAR

20-INCHES SAUSAGE CASING, RUBBED
   WITH SALT AND RINSED

APPROX. 2 CUPS PEANUT OR CORN OIL
   FOR DEEP-FRYING

serves 4 to 6

METHOD

Mix the pork, rice, lime juice, garlic, salt, pepper, and sugar well. Stuff into the sausage casing, and tie along the length with string into small balls. Chill in the refrigerator for 24 hours. Prick the sausage with a toothpick. Heat the oil to 180°C in a pan, and fry the sausage on both sides until brown and well cooked, about 15 minutes. Cut into individual sausages. Serve accompanied by fresh sliced ginger, fresh cabbage, fresh small green chilies, peanuts, scallions and cilantro leaves.

Jazzed Cecils – ENGLAND

METHOD

Combine the meat, onion, bread crumbs, garlic, tomato paste, sugar, paprika, Tabasco, herbs, and egg, and season. Mold the mixture into small balls about the size of a large marble, and roll in the seasoned flour. Fry them in the butter and oil for 5 to 10 minutes. Drain on paper towels, and keep warm. To make the dip, mix together the yogurt, chives, and parsley, and season to taste. Serve the cecils with toothpicks and the yogurt dip.

INGREDIENTS

4 CUPS GROUND BEEF

1 SMALL ONION, GRATED

1 CUP FRESH WHITE BREAD CRUMBS

2–3 GARLIC CLOVES, CRUSHED

2 TEASPOONS TOMATO PASTE

1 TEASPOON SUGAR

1 TEASPOON PAPRIKA

2 DASHES OF TABASCO

1 EGG, BEATEN

SALT AND FRESHLY GROUND
   BLACK PEPPER

½ CUP SEASONED ALL-PURPOSE FLOUR

¼ CUP BUTTER

2 TABLESPOONS OIL

FOR THE DIP

1 CUP THICK YOGURT

1 TABLESPOON CHOPPED FRESH CHIVES

1 TABLESPOON CHOPPED FRESH PARSLEY

serves 4 to 6

Spiced Fruit Meatballs – LEBANON

Mouth-watering meatballs such as these occur in many variations throughout the Middle East. The inclusion of fruit is a preference of Turkey and the Levant, where the mingling of savory and sweet is more common. Currants or dates can be substituted for the golden raisins.

METHOD

Mix together the bread crumbs and yogurt in a bowl, and let soak for 10 minutes. Heat 1 tablespoon of the oil in a skillet and sauté the pine nuts until lightly golden, about 4 to 5 minutes. Drain on paper towels, and add to the yogurt mix. Stir in the golden raisins, scallions, garlic, spices, and salt. Add the meat, and combine thoroughly using your hands. Chill the meat mixture for 30 minutes. Make about thirty small balls from the mixture. Heat the oil, and sauté the balls in batches for about 6 minutes, turning to make sure they brown all over. Transfer to paper towels to drain, and keep warm while cooking the remaining balls. The balls may be refrigerated or frozen and reheated in the oven when required.

INGREDIENTS

1 CUP FRESH WHITE BREAD CRUMBS

½ CUP YOGURT

3 TABLESPOONS OLIVE OIL

½ CUP PINE NUTS

⅓ CUP GOLDEN RAISINS, SULTANAS
   SOAKED IN HOT WATER AND DRAINED

3 TABLESPOONS FINELY CHOPPED
   SCALLIONS

1 GARLIC CLOVE, FINELY CHOPPED

1 TEASPOON GROUND CINNAMON

1 TEASPOON GROUND ALLSPICE

1 TEASPOON SALT

4 CUPS GROUND LAMB OR BEEF

1 TABLESPOON OIL

makes 25 to 30

CHAPTER FOUR

Cold

Appetizers

~

Potato Omelet – SPAIN

INGREDIENTS

½ CUP OLIVE OIL

1 POUND POTATOES, DICED

6 LARGE EGGS

SALT AND FRESHLY GROUND BLACK
   PEPPER

serves 4

Virtually every *tapas* bar and menu in Spain offers this dish. It should be thick, firm and cake-like, quite unlike the French omelet.

METHOD

A pan about 9 inches in diameter is right for this dish (a bigger one makes the omelet difficult to turn). Heat the oil well, add the potatoes and stir them. After a couple of minutes reduce the heat, and let the potatoes cook through, turning frequently so they do not color. Move them to a bowl with paper towels at the bottom. Drain the oil from the pan into a cup, and wipe out the pan with paper towels. Strain about 2 tablespoons of the oil back into the pan and reheat. Beat the eggs together, and season them well. Remove the paper from beneath the potatoes, and pour in the eggs. Pour this mixture into the hot oil, spreading the potatoes evenly, and let the omelet set for a minute at high heat. Turn down the heat to cook through. Use a spatula to work round the pan edge, and shake the pan to and fro occasionally, to stop the omelet sticking underneath. When the top has ceased to be liquid, cover with a serving plate and invert the pan to turn out. Add 2 tablespoons of the oil from the cup to the pan, reheat it and return the omelet, cooked side up, to the pan, and cook for 2 to 3 minutes longer. Spanish omelet can be served hot or cold as a tapa, a main course, or a sandwich filling.

Meze Mushrooms — GREECE

This *meze* dish is best kept simple, with the use of fresh, firm mushrooms and a good-quality olive oil for the best flavor.

INGREDIENTS

⅔ CUP OLIVE OIL

½ CUP DRY WHITE WINE

SALT AND FRESHLY GROUND
    BLACK PEPPER

1 TEASPOON DRIED THYME

3 GARLIC CLOVES, CRUSHED

4 TABLESPOONS CHOPPED FRESH
    PARSLEY

1¼ POUNDS TINY BUTTON
    MUSHROOMS

JUICE OF 1 LEMON

CHOPPED FRESH PARSLEY, TO GARNISH

serves 6 to 8

METHOD

Place all the ingredients, except the mushrooms and half the lemon juice, in a large saucepan, and bring to a boil. Reduce the heat, and stir in the mushrooms. Cover and simmer for 8 to 10 minutes. Transfer the mushrooms and the liquid to a serving dish, and let cool completely. Serve at room temperature, sprinkled with the remaining lemon juice and garnished with chopped fresh parsley.

Avocados with Cauliflower and Bacon — SPAIN

INGREDIENTS

2 RIPE AVOCADOS

½ CUP GOOD QUALITY MAYONNAISE

1 GARLIC CLOVE, FINELY CRUSHED

8 SLICES BACON, CUT INTO
    ½-INCH PIECES

8 OUNCES RAW CAULIFLOWER FLORETS

serves 4

METHOD

Halve and pit the avocados. Widen and deepen the cavity a little by scraping out about ½ tablespoon of flesh from each. Mash the scraped out avocado flesh with the mayonnaise, and stir in the crushed garlic. Broil or fry the bacon until crisp. Mix the dressing with the cauliflower florets and most of the bacon, and pile the mixture into the avocado halves. Crumble the remaining bacon, and sprinkle over the top. Serve immediately or the cut avocado will turn brown.

Crispy "Seaweed" – CHINA

You might be surprised or even shocked to learn that the very popular "seaweed" served in Chinese restaurants is, in fact, green cabbage! Choose fresh, young cabbage with pointed heads. Even the deep green outer leaves are quite tender. This recipe also makes an ideal garnish for a number of dishes, particularly cold appetizers and buffet dishes.

INGREDIENTS

1½–1¼ POUNDS YOUNG CABBAGE

2½ CUPS OIL FOR DEEP-FRYING

1 TEASPOON SALT

1 TEASPOON SUGAR

serves 4

METHOD

Wash and dry the cabbage leaves, and shred them with a sharp knife into the thinnest possible shavings. Spread them out on paper towels, or put in a large colander to dry thoroughly. Heat the oil in a wok or deep-fryer. Before the oil gets too hot, turn off the heat for 30 seconds. Add the cabbage shavings in several batches, and turn the heat up to medium high. Stir with a pair of cooking chopsticks. When the shavings start to float to the surface, scoop them out gently with a slotted spoon, and drain on paper towels to remove as much of the oil as possible. Sprinkle the salt and sugar evenly on top, and mix gently. Serve cold.

Variation

Deep-fry ½ cup split almonds until crisp, and add to the "seaweed" as a garnish, to give the dish a new dimension.

Barbados-style Pickled Fish – CARIBBEAN

METHOD

Put the onions, carrots, green bell peppers, bay leaves, chili, salt and pepper to taste, plus the vinegar, 1½ tablespoons of the oil and the water into a large saucepan, and bring to a boil over a high heat. Reduce the heat, and simmer until the vegetables are cooked. Meanwhile, pour the remaining oil into a large skillet, and heat. Add the fish fillets, and cook each side for 2 minutes or until golden brown. Transfer the fish to a shallow heatproof dish. Pour the contents of the saucepan over the fish, and let cool. Serve with baked yams or breadfruit.

INGREDIENTS

4 ONIONS, THINLY SLICED

2 CARROTS, SCRAPED AND SLICED

2 GREEN BELL PEPPERS, SEEDED AND
   CHOPPED

2 BAY LEAVES

½ TEASPOON CRUSHED FRESH CHILI

2 TEASPOONS SALT

FRESHLY GROUND BLACK PEPPER

6 TABLESPOONS WHITE WINE VINEGAR

5 TABLESPOONS OLIVE OIL

1¼ CUPS COLD WATER

2 POUNDS RED SNAPPER, SKINNED AND
   FILLETED

serves 6

Smoked Salmon and Pasta Cocktails — ITALY

INGREDIENTS

4 OUNCES FRESH PASTA SPIRALS

4 TABLESPOONS MAYONNAISE

4 TABLESPOONS SOUR CREAM

2 TABLESPOONS SNIPPED FRESH CHIVES

SALT AND FRESHLY GROUND
    BLACK PEPPER

4 CHICORY OR FRISÉE LEAVES, COARSELY
    SHREDDED

6 OUNCES SMOKED SALMON,
    SHREDDED

2 TABLESPOONS CHOPPED DILL

GRATED RIND OF ½ LEMON

DILL SPRIGS, TO GARNISH

4 LEMON WEDGES, TO SERVE

serves 4

This turns a comparatively small quantity of smoked salmon into an attractive appetizer.

METHOD

Cook the pasta in boiling salted water for 3 minutes. Drain and cool. Mix the mayonnaise, sour cream, and chives with the pasta. Add seasoning to taste. Arrange the chicory or frisée in four glass dishes, then divide the pasta between

the dishes. Mix the smoked salmon with the dill and lemon rind, then arrange the shreds on top of the pasta. Garnish with dill sprigs. Serve lemon wedges with the cocktails so that their

Gazpacho Aspic — AMERICA

INGREDIENTS

8 OUNCES RIPE TOMATOES, SEEDED AND
    CHOPPED

⅔ CUP FINELY CHOPPED GREEN BELL
    PEPPER

½ CUP DICED CUCUMBER

2 SCALLIONS, CHOPPED, GREEN AND
    WHITE PARTS SEPARATED

2 TEASPOONS CHOPPED FRESH CILANTRO

2 TEASPOONS CHOPPED FRESH BASIL

1 GARLIC CLOVE, CRUSHED

2 ENVELOPES POWDERED GELATIN

1½ CUPS CANNED TOMATO JUICE

1 CUP CHICKEN STOCK

FINELY DICED CELERY

1 TEASPOON SALT

½ TEASPOON WORCESTERSHIRE SAUCE

DASH OF TABASCO SAUCE

serves 6

Gazpacho aspic is a cool way to eat your vegetables on a hot day. Raid the garden for fresh vegetables, and make this aspic early in the day. Some of the vegetables are puréed, and some are added in their chopped form to make a chunky aspic. Like gazpacho soup, you can spice it up with extra Tabasco if you like your food spicy. The aspic is good plain, but you can also dress it up with a little herb mayonnaise.

METHOD

Purée the tomatoes, one-third of the green pepper, half the cucumber, the white part of the scallions, cilantro, basil, and garlic. Set aside. Pour ½ cup of the tomato juice into a small bowl, and sprinkle the gelatin over it. While the gelatin is dissolving, heat the remaining tomato juice, chicken stock and purée in a medium saucepan. If the gelatin begins to set, put some water in a shallow pan, and set the bowl in the pan. The

water should not come near the top of the bowl. Put the pan over low heat. The gelatin will dissolve. Add the puréed mixture to the aspic mixture, and bring it to a boil. Remove from the heat, and add the celery, vegetables, salt, Worcestershire sauce and Tabasco. Pour into a 1-cup mold or bowl. Refrigerate for 4 hours, or until set.

Stuffed Tomatoes – SPAIN

INGREDIENTS

8 REGULAR TOMATOES, OR 3 BEEF
  TOMATOES

4 HARD-COOKED EGGS, COOLED AND
  SHELLED

6 TABLESPOONS GARLIC MAYONNAISE

SALT AND FRESHLY GROUND BLACK
  PEPPER

1 TABLESPOON CHOPPED FRESH PARSLEY,
  TO GARNISH

1 TABLESPOON WHITE BREAD CRUMBS
  FOR THE BEEF TOMATOES

serves 8 or 6

You can use small tomatoes or large beef tomatoes for this recipe, which is very simple and a colorful addition to any table.

METHOD

Peel the tomatoes, first by cutting out the core with a sharp knife and making a "+" incision on the other end of the tomato. Then place in a pan of boiling water for 10 seconds, remove and plunge into a bowl of ice or very cold water (this latter step is to stop the tomatoes from cooking and going mushy). Slice the tops off the tomatoes, and just enough of their bottoms to remove the rounded ends so that the tomatoes will sit squarely on the plate. Keep the tops if using small tomatoes, but not for the large tomatoes. Remove the seeds and cores, either with a teaspoon or small, sharp knife. Mash the eggs with the mayonnaise, salt, pepper, and parsley. Fill the tomatoes, firmly pressing the filling down. With small tomatoes, replace the lids at an angle. If keeping to serve later, brush them with olive oil and black pepper to prevent from drying out. Cover with platic wrap and keep. For large tomatoes, the filling must be very firm, so it can be sliced. If you make your own mayonnaise, thicken it by using more egg yolks. If you use store-bought mayonnaise, add enough white bread crumbs until the mixture is the consistency of mashed potatoes. Season well, to taste. Fill the tomatoes, pressing down firmly until level. Refrigerate for 1 hour, then slice with a sharp carving knife into rings. Sprinkle with chopped parsley.

Stuffed Cabbage Rolls — RUSSIAN FEDERATION

INGREDIENTS

2½–3 POUNDS WHITE DANISH OR
   SAVOY CABBAGE

3 TABLESPOONS BUTTER

1 TABLESPOON OIL

2 LARGE ONIONS, FINELY CHOPPED

4 CUPS LEAN GROUND BEEF

2 CUPS LEAN GROUND VEAL

1½ CUPS COOKED LONG-GRAIN WHITE
   RICE

1 EGG, BEATEN

SALT AND FRESHLY GROUND BLACK
   PEPPER

6 SLICES BACON

1 x 14-OUNCE CAN CHOPPED
   TOMATOES

½ CUP BEEF STOCK

1 TABLESPOON ALL-PURPOSE FLOUR

⅔ CUP SOUR CREAM

1 CUP FINELY CHOPPED FRESH DILL

serves 8

Cabbage rolls are made by Russians, Poles, Czechs and Hungarians, though each version has special spices and ingredients. The Hungarian one makes use of paprika, while typical recipes from the Ukraine – where they are called holubsti – contain mushrooms and are often meatless.

METHOD

Bring a large saucepan or casserole of water to a boil. Lower in the whole head of cabbage. Cover and cook for about 8 minutes. Remove the cabbage, but keep the water on a boil. Carefully remove as many leaves as you can without tearing them. Return the cabbage to the saucepan, and cook for a little longer, then remove and again detach as many leaves as you can. Repeat the process until you have twenty or so large leaves. Trim each leaf, removing the toughest part of the central stalk. Set aside. Heat the butter and oil in a skillet, and sauté the onion until it is softened and golden. Transfer to a large bowl, and add the beef, veal, cooked rice, egg, and seasoning to taste. Mix with your hands until thoroughly combined. Lay 3 to 4 leaves out, and place about 3 tablespoons of filling on each.

Roll up from the stalk end, turning in the sides, and finish at the leaf end to make a neat package. If necessary, secure with a wooden toothpick. Place the packets seam-side down in a shallow casserole large enough to hold all the rolls in one layer. Lay the bacon slices over the rolls. Preheat the oven to 350°F. In a saucepan heat together the chopped tomatoes and beef stock. Remove 2 tablespoons to mix with the flour in a bowl. Whisk in the sour cream and dill, and return the mixture to the hot tomato-beef stock mixture, stirring. Season to taste, and pour the sauce over the cabbage rolls. Bake the rolls, uncovered, for 1 hour or until the sauce is bubbling and the rolls are slightly browned. Let rest for 10 minutes before serving.

Sorbet Tomatoes – ENGLAND

INGREDIENTS

2 LARGE BEEF TOMATOES

PINCH OF SALT

2 GARLIC CLOVES, CRUSHED

FRESHLY GROUND BLACK PEPPER

A GENEROUS HANDFUL OF FRESH MINT
  LEAVES

JUICE OF 1 LARGE LEMON

2 TEASPOONS SUGAR

2 EGG WHITES

SPRIGS OF FRESH MINT, TO SERVE

serves 4

METHOD

Halve the tomatoes horizontally, scoop out and reserve the seeds and cores. Sprinkle the insides of the tomato shells with a little salt, and turn upside down to drain. Smear the inside of each tomato shell with the crushed garlic, and sprinkle with plenty of pepper. Press the tomato seeds and cores through a strainer to extract the juice, and make up to ⅔ cup with water. Combine the mint leaves, tomato juice, lemon juice, and sugar in a blender or food processor. The mixture should not be too smooth. Pack into an ice-cube tray, and freeze for about an hour, until crystalline but still slightly mushy. Beat the egg whites with a couple of pinches of salt until they form soft peaks, and fold into the semi-frozen mint mixture. Freeze until firm, stirring occasionally. Pile the sorbet into each tomato half, and garnish with a sprig of mint.

Moorish Pickled Anchovies – SPAIN

INGREDIENTS

2¼ POUNDS FRESH ANCHOVIES, OR
  SARDINES OR SMELTS, ETC.

6–8 TABLESPOONS OLIVE OIL

½ CUP ALL-PURPOSE FLOUR

SALT AND FRESHLY GROUND BLACK
  PEPPER

6 GARLIC CLOVES, FINELY CHOPPED

SMALL PINCH OF SAFFRON STRANDS

1 TEASPOON CUMIN SEEDS

1 TEASPOON GROUND GINGER

1 CUP RED WINE VINEGAR

4 BAY LEAVES

1 LEMON, THINLY SLICED

serves 8

METHOD

Cut off the fish heads, pulling out their innards. Slit them down the belly, as far as the tail, and swish the insides under a faucet. Then put each fish down on a board, black back upwards, and press a thumb firmly down on it. This opens it out like a book and makes it easy to rip out the backbone and tail. Heat 4 tablespoons of oil in a large skillet. Dust the fish with seasoned flour on a baking sheet and fry immediately you have a sheetful (there will be about four of these). Put them in skin-side down and turn after 1 to 2 minutes. Transfer them to paper towels to drain. Take the pan off the heat between batches, and add more oil as necessary. Fry the garlic in the remaining oil, then transfer to a mortar or a small herb (or coffee) mill. Work to a paste with a pinch of salt, the saffron, cumin seeds, and ginger. Work in the vinegar. Arrange the fish in an earthenware dish, skin-side up. This can be shallow if you are planning to serve them within 24 hours, but should be smaller and deeper if you want to keep them. Mix 1 cup of water into the spicy mixture, and pour this over the fish. Add more vinegar and water to cover them completely if you are keeping them. Lay the bay leaves and very thinly sliced lemon over the top. Refrigerate for half a day before eating. They can be served straight from the dish. They should be eaten within a week.

Smoked Salmon-stuffed Tomatoes – IRELAND

METHOD

Preheat the oven to 350°F. Cut the tops off the tomatoes. Scoop out the insides, throw away the centers and seeds, and place the tomato pulp in a bowl. Chop the shallots and the onion finely, and mix with the tomato pulp. Purée the smoked salmon, and add to the bowl. Chop the dill finely, place in the bowl with the smoked salmon and all the remaining ingredients. Mix well. Spoon the mixture back into the tomatoes, put the tomato tops on, and bake for about 20 minutes. Serve on a bed of watercress. These stuffed tomatoes are good hot or cold.

INGREDIENTS

8 MEDIUM-SIZED TOMATOES

2 SHALLOTS

1 SPANISH ONION

8 OUNCES SMOKED SALMON

BUNCH OF FRESH DILL

2 CUPS FRESH BREAD CRUMBS

1 LEMON

1 TABLESPOON LIGHT CREAM

1 TABLESPOON TABASCO SAUCE

BUNCH OF WATERCRESS, TO SERVE

serves 8

Shrimp in Garlic and Herbs – SPAIN

INGREDIENTS

1 CUP OLIVE OIL

1 PINT SHRIMP, SHELLED; IF USING
    FROZEN, COOK

2 TABLESPOONS CRUSHED GARLIC

1½ TABLESPOONS CHOPPED FRESH
    PARSLEY

1½ TABLESPOONS CHOPPED FRESH
    CILANTRO

SALT AND FRESHLY GROUND
    BLACK PEPPER

3 LEMONS, CUT INTO WEDGES, TO SERVE

serves 4

METHOD

Heat the oil in a pot. Add the shrimp, cover, lower the heat and cook for 2 minutes, until the heat goes through them. Add the garlic, herbs, salt and pepper. Stir and cook for 2 minutes longer. Serve in small bowls with lemon wedges.

Jamaican Papaya Crab – CARIBBEAN

INGREDIENTS

2 RIPE PAPAYAS, ABOUT 10 OUNCES
    EACH

2 TABLESPOONS WHIPPED CREAM

½ CUP MAYONNAISE

GARLIC JUICE, TO TASTE

JUICE OF LIME OR LEMON

A LITTLE GROUND WHITE PEPPER

2½ CUPS CRAB MEAT

serves 4

According to Jamaican folklore, a goat tied to a papaya tree won't be there in the morning. This luxurious combination of papaya and crab meat will disappear a lot quicker.

METHOD

Split the papayas, and remove the seeds and "strings." Mix the whipped cream with the mayonnaise. As homemade mayonnaise is so much richer than a commercial brand, you may need to add a little more whipped cream to lighten it. Flavor to taste with garlic juice, lime or lemon juice, and a little white pepper. This dressing should be delicate. Combine the dressing with the crab meat, and pile into papaya halves. Serve chilled.

Variation

For Melon Crab, use two small melons, halved and deseeded, instead of the papayas. The fragrant, orange- or peach-fleshed varieties of melon, such as Charentais and cantaloupe, are particularly good for this.

Pickled Fish – PERU

This very contemporary fish dish, also known as ceviche, is popular with Jews in Central and South America. Any firm white fish can be used, as well as salmon, sea trout and even thinly sliced scallops. The acid in the lime and lemon juice has a similar effect to heat; the fish is effectively cooked.

METHOD

Cut the fish fillets into 1-inch strips; place in a large, shallow non-metallic dish. In a large bowl, combine the remaining ingredients, except garnish. Pour the marinade over the fish strips, spreading evenly over the fish. Refrigerate for at least 3 hours, or until the fish strips turn white and opaque. (Do not marinate much longer or the fish will begin to fall apart as the acids continue to break down the proteins.) Serve a few fish strips with some chili and onion slices on individual plates, and garnish with cilantro leaves.

INGREDIENTS

2 POUNDS SOLE, HALIBUT OR
   RED SNAPPER FILLETS, OR ANY
   COMBINATION OF FIRM-FLESHED
   NON-OILY FISH

1 CUP LEMON JUICE

1 CUP LIME JUICE

2 FRESH RED CHILIES, THINLY SLICED

2 RED ONIONS, THINLY SLICED

1 TO 2 GARLIC CLOVES, PEELED AND
   FINELY CHOPPED

ROCK SALT

FRESHLY GROUND BLACK PEPPER

FRESH CILANTRO LEAVES, TO GARNISH

serves 4 to 6

Marinated Whitebait – SPAIN

INGREDIENTS

1 POUND FROZEN WHITEBAIT,
   DEFROSTED (FOR ABOUT 2 HOURS AT
   ROOM TEMPERATURE)

1 TABLESPOON CHOPPED FRESH PARSLEY

2 TEASPOONS CRUSHED GARLIC

2 TEASPOONS FRESHLY GROUND BLACK
   PEPPER

JUICE OF 2 LEMONS (OR ENOUGH
   TO COVER THE FISH WHILE
   THEY MARINATE)

2 SHALLOTS, FINELY CHOPPED

1 TEASPOON FRESHLY GROUND BLACK
   PEPPER

½ TEASPOON SALT

4 TABLESPOONS OLIVE OIL

serves 4

METHOD

Remove the heads of the whitebait. Split the larger ones lengthwise, leave the small ones whole. Pull out the bones of the larger ones. Place on a baking sheet or in a square dish (not a metal dish). Cover with the parsley, garlic, lemon juice, shallots, and seasoning. Let marinate for 24 hours in the refrigerator. Drain off the excess juice. Cover with the oil, leave for 1 hour and then serve.

Tuna Fish with Garbanzo Beans – GREECE

This wonderful, summery combination of tuna fish and garbanzo beans makes an excellent cold *meze* dish. It's also a quick, easy and nutritious idea for a light lunch.

METHOD

Drain the garbanzo beans and tuna fish, and place in a medium-sized bowl. Gently stir in the scallions and celery. Combine the oil, lemon juice and rind, parsley, dill, salt and pepper, garlic, and mustard powder all together in a screw-top jar. Shake well to mix, then pour over the beans and tuna fish. Stir gently to combine, then turn the mixture out onto a serving plate. Cover and chill for several hours before serving, for the best results. Garnish with fresh herbs.

INGREDIENTS

14-OUNCE CAN GARBANZO BEANS
2 x 7-OUNCE CANS TUNA FISH IN BRINE
4 SCALLIONS, FINELY CHOPPED
1 CELERY STALK, FINELY CHOPPED
½ CUP OLIVE OIL
4 TABLESPOONS LEMON JUICE
FINELY GRATED RIND OF ½ LEMON
3 TABLESPOONS CHOPPED FRESH
    PARSLEY
1 TABLESPOON CHOPPED FRESH DILL
SALT AND FRESHLY GROUND
    BLACK PEPPER
2 GARLIC CLOVES, CRUSHED
¼ TEASPOON MUSTARD POWDER
FRESH PARSLEY AND DILL, TO GARNISH

serves 4 to 6

Grenada-style Oyster Cocktail – CARIBBEAN

METHOD

Rinse the oysters under cold running water, then let them soak in a bowl of cold water with 1 teaspoon of the lime juice for 5 minutes. Drain off the water. In a bowl, mix the remaining lime juice with the Tabasco sauce, onion, salt, tomato, and olive oil. Add the oysters, and let marinate for 5 minutes. Chill for 10 minutes before serving.

INGREDIENTS

24 FRESH OYSTERS
4 TEASPOONS LIME JUICE
½ TEASPOON TABASCO SAUCE
1 ONION, FINELY CHOPPED
2 TEASPOONS SALT
1 SMALL, FRESH TOMATO, PEELED AND
    FINELY CHOPPED
1 TEASPOON OLIVE OIL

serves 6

Seviche – MEXICO

INGREDIENTS

1 POUND FIRM WHITE FISH FILLETS, SKINNED AND CUBED

½ CUP LIME JUICE

1 SMALL ONION, FINELY CHOPPED

1 LARGE TOMATO, PEELED, SEEDED AND CHOPPED

1–2 FRESH GREEN CHILIES, SEEDED AND THINLY SLICED

3 TABLESPOONS OLIVE OIL

PINCH OF SALT

1 SMALL RIPE AVOCADO, PEELED, PITTED AND SLICED (OPTIONAL)

serves 4

METHOD

Put the fish into a pretty glass bowl, and pour the lime juice over it. Cover and let marinate for 4 to 6 hours or overnight. Half an hour or so before serving, stir in the remaining ingredients, except for the avocado, and season to taste. Chill briefly, and serve garnished with avocado slices, if you like.

Sardine-stuffed Lemons – LEBANON

INGREDIENTS

3 PLUMP ROUND LEMONS

2 x 5-OUNCE CANS SARDINES PACKED IN OIL, DRAINED

3 TABLESPOONS MAYONNAISE

1½ TABLESPOONS DIJON MUSTARD

1 LARGE CELERY STALK, FINELY CHOPPED

4 SCALLIONS, FINELY CHOPPED

2 TABLESPOONS FINELY CHOPPED FLAT-LEAFED PARSLEY

SALT AND FRESHLY GROUND PEPPER

2 TABLESPOONS TOASTED PINE NUTS, TO GARNISH

GREEN OLIVES, CUT LENGTHWISE INTO SLIVERS, TO GARNISH

serves 6

Sardines, like lentils, are a traditional food of the poor, which now have considerable cachet among the foodies. Coastal Lebanon has always appreciated them, however, usually simply broiled or stuffed and baked. This is a different presentation, eaten as a light lunch or a European-style first course.

METHOD

Halve the lemons and squeeze them with a juicer; reserve the juice. Carefully cut a thin slice from the bottom of each so that it will stand. With your fingers, try to remove as much as possible of the inner membrane from each half. Place the halves upside down for a few minutes. Meanwhile place the drained sardines in a bowl. Mash together with the mayonnaise, mustard, and 2 tablespoons of the lemon juice. Try to obtain a fairly smooth paste. Work in the chopped celery, scallions, and parsley. Season to taste, and give a final stir. Divide the sardine paste among the six lemon halves, shape the tops attractively, and garnish with a few toasted pine nuts and slivers of green olive. Chill briefly (for up to 2 hours) and serve with warm Arab or pocket bread.

Chicken with Apricots and Olives – LEBANON

INGREDIENTS

3½ POUND CHICKEN, SKINNED,
  BONELESS AND CUBED

5 GARLIC CLOVES, CRUSHED

¾ CUP CHOPPED READY-TO-EAT DRIED
  APRICOTS

⅓ CUP BLACK GREEK OLIVES

½ TEASPOON GRATED ORANGE PEEL

5 TABLESPOONS ORANGE JUICE

2 TABLESPOONS LEMON JUICE OR WHITE
  WINE VINEGAR

½ CUP ARAK (ANISE-BASED LEBANESE
  LIQUEUR) OR OUZO

2 TABLESPOONS FRESH FENNEL LEAVES

1½ TABLESPOONS OLIVE OIL

⅔ CUP LIGHT BROWN SUGAR

serves 8

This savory combination owes more to the Israeli taste than to classic Lebanese cuisine. Israel is Europe's richest source of dried fruits, and they make a frequent appearance in the meat stews and desserts of that country. However, taste cannot be confined by national borders, and dishes like this one have become common in Lebanon.

METHOD

Preheat the oven to 400°F. Combine all the ingredients except the sugar in a large bowl, and stir carefully to mix well. Cover and chill overnight. Transfer the chicken pieces to a baking pan, and pour over the marinade, including the olives and apricots. Sprinkle over the sugar. Bake for about 30 minutes, turning once or twice.

Remove the chicken pieces to a serving platter, and arrange the olives and apricots over and around them. Strain the cooking juices into a saucepan, and reduce over high heat to about half. Pour the sauce over the chicken. Serve warm or cold.

Spinach and Ham Omelet – ITALY

INGREDIENTS

6 EGGS

3 TABLESPOONS FRESHLY GRATED
  PARMESAN CHEESE

¾ CUP COARSELY CHOPPED PROSCIUTTO

1 CUP COOKED SPINACH

SALT AND FRESHLY GROUND
  BLACK PEPPER

4 TABLESPOONS OLIVE OIL

serves 4

The Italian omelet is not the light and runny affair of France, but a thick, multi-egged and completely cooked number, served in wedges like a cake, often cold. Such dishes may be eaten at the evening meal, which in Italy is traditionally much lighter than lunch.

METHOD

Thoroughly beat the eggs. Mix in the cheese, ham, spinach, salt and pepper. Heat the oil over a medium flame, in as heavy a pan as you have. Pour in the mixture, and then turn the heat down as low as it will go. Cover the pan, and cook until everything is set – about 20 minutes. Serve at whatever temperature you wish.

Fava Beans with Ham, Ronda-style – SPAIN

So popular is this fresh fava bean dish all over Spain that it is sometimes called española instead. It is made with raw serrano ham – the sierras of Ronda are famous for their hams from the black-footed pig. Another virtue is that it is attractive made with frozen beans. In summer, when parsley is almost unobtainable in the south, the garnish may be diced red bell pepper or tomato.

METHOD

Fry the onion in the oil in a flameproof casserole. As it starts to soften, add the ham or bacon and garlic, and fry until lightly browned. Stir in the beans (frozen beans need no water; fresh ones need ½ cup). Cover, and simmer until tender, stirring occasionally. Fresh or frozen, they take about 10 minutes. Season the beans generously, stir in the chopped eggs, and heat through. Stir in the parsley and serve.

INGREDIENTS

1 CUP CHOPPED SPANISH OR BERMUDA ONION

4 TABLESPOONS OLIVE OIL

1¼ CUPS DICED RAW HAM OR CANADIAN BACON

1 GARLIC CLOVE, FINELY CHOPPED

2¼ POUNDS YOUNG, PODDED (OR FROZEN) FAVA BEANS

SALT AND FRESHLY GROUND BLACK PEPPER

4 HARD-COOKED EGGS, SHELLED AND CHOPPED

1 CUP CHOPPED FRESH PARSLEY

serves 6

Sour Orange Turkey – LEBANON

The turkeys that roam unfettered in the Levant are a small black-necked breed, tasty but not always tender. This sour marinade tenderizes the meat while lending a tangy fruitiness. Sour oranges were brought to southern Europe by the Arabs, where they became better known as "Seville oranges."

INGREDIENTS

10–12 POUND TURKEY

6 SEVILLE ORANGES

4 GARLIC CLOVES, CUT INTO SLIVERS

3 RED OR MILD YELLOW ONIONS

2 TABLESPOONS FINELY CHOPPED FRESH
   MARJORAM

¼ CUP OLIVE OIL

1 TEASPOON GROUND CORIANDER

SALT AND FRESHLY GROUND PEPPER

FLAT-LEAFED PARSLEY

½ CUP PLAIN YOGURT (OPTIONAL)

serves 8

METHOD

Wash the turkey, and pat it dry with paper towels. Squeeze the juice from four oranges, and reserve the other two. Make small gashes through the turkey skin into the flesh, and insert the garlic slivers into them. Slice two of the onions thinly into a large enamel-lined casserole, and place the turkey on top. Scatter the marjoram on top, and pour over the orange juice. Cover the bowl and chill for one day, turning the turkey several times in the marinade. Preheat the oven to 400°F. Take the turkey from the marinade, and pat it dry. Rub all over with the olive oil, ground coriander, and salt and pepper to taste. Remove the sliced onions from the marinade with a slotted spoon, and arrange them over the bottom of a baking pan. Place the turkey on top, breast-side down, and pour over the marinade. Roast in the oven for 10 minutes, then lower the heat to 325°F, and continue roasting, basting with the pan juices occasionally, for 2½ hours longer, or until the juices run clear when the turkey is pierced with a skewer or sharp knife. If necessary, add some water to the liquid to keep it from drying out. Remove the bird from the oven, place on a serving platter, and let it rest, covered, for 15 minutes. Strain the pan juices into a saucepan. Peel the two remaining oranges, separate them into segments, and add to the saucepan. Reduce the sauce over a high heat until it thickens slightly. Cut the turkey meat into serving pieces, slice the breast, and arrange on the serving platter. Slice the last onion, and arrange the rings over the turkey pieces. Strain over the reduced juices and orange segments. Garnish with flat-leafed parsley, and serve immediately. The turkey may also be served cold with yogurt. Whisk some of the reduced juices and finely chopped parsley into the yogurt before chilling it.

Farmyard Chicken with Olives — SPAIN

This is a favorite dish because sherry and olives set off the flavor of the chicken so well. It is good served hot from the casserole, but better still jellied. Cutting up the chicken first means it takes less time to cook and improves the quality of the sauce, because it reduces the amount of liquid. In Spain it is served with bread, but rice (hot or cold) could also be used.

METHOD

Fry the onions in the oil in a casserole, adding the garlic when they soften. Salt and pepper the chicken portions, and pack these neatly into the pan, with the backbone, putting the olives in the spaces. Add the sherry and bay leaves, and pour in water to almost cover (about 1½ cups). Simmer, covered, for 30 to 35 minutes. Spoon the chicken from the casserole, let cool for a few minutes, then remove the bones and skin.

Return these to the liquid, and boil for 10 minutes longer to strengthen the jelly and increase its flavor. Check the seasonings. Meanwhile, split the cooked chicken into large pieces, arrange them in a shallow dish, and distribute the olives. Strain the juices into a bowl, and skim off all fat. Pour over the chicken, and chill until the jelly has set.

INGREDIENTS

2 ONIONS, CHOPPED

2 TABLESPOONS OLIVE OIL

3 GARLIC CLOVES, CHOPPED

SALT AND FRESHLY GROUND
   BLACK PEPPER

2¼-POUND CORN-FED CHICKEN,
   QUARTERED AND BACKBONE FREED

24 GREEN OLIVES

¼ CUP FINO SHERRY
   OR MONTILLA

2 BAY LEAVES

serves 4

5

Hot

Appetizers

~

Glossy Dumplings – CHINA

INGREDIENTS

2 CHINESE DRIED MUSHROOMS

GENEROUS 1 CUP LEAN GROUND PORK

1 TABLESPOON FINELY CHOPPED FRESH
  GINGER ROOT

1 GARLIC CLOVE, CRUSHED

1 TEASPOON SESAME OIL

2 TABLESPOONS FINELY CHOPPED WATER
  CHESTNUTS OR CELERY

2 SCALLIONS, FINELY CHOPPED

2 TABLESPOONS SOY SAUCE

PINCH OF FIVE-SPICE POWDER

SCALLION CURLS, TO GARNISH

FOR THE DOUGH

1 CUP BREAD FLOUR

2 TABLESPOONS LARD

FOR THE DIPPING SAUCES

1 GARLIC CLOVE, FINELY CHOPPED

1 TEASPOON FINELY CHOPPED FRESH
  GINGER ROOT

1 TABLESPOON FINELY CHOPPED
  SCALLION

1 TABLESPOON DRY SHERRY

ABOUT 1 CUP SOY SAUCE

serves 12

METHOD

Place the mushrooms in a cup. Add just enough boiling water to cover them, then put a small saucer over them, and weight it down to keep the mushrooms submerged. Let stand for 20 minutes. Mix the pork, ginger, garlic, sesame oil, water chestnuts or celery, scallions, soy sauce and five-spice powder. Drain the mushrooms, discard any woody stalks, then chop the caps finely. Add them to the pork, and mix the ingredients thoroughly. To make the dough, place the flour in a basin. Measure ¼ cup boiling water, and stir in the lard. When the lard has melted, pour the mixture into the flour, and stir well to form a soft dough. Sprinkle a little cornstarch on the work surface, and knead the dough lightly; then roll it into a sausage, and mark it into 24 pieces. Cut off a piece of dough to shape, then loosely cover the rest of the roll with plastic wrap. Knead the dough briefly into a smooth ball, then flatten it into a round measuring about 2 to 2½ inches across. Place a little of the meat mixture in the middle, then fold the dough over it to make a tiny dumpling in the shape of a Cornish pasty. Pinch and flute the edges to seal in the filling. Grease a shallow dish or plate, and place the dumpling on it. Flatten and fill the remaining dough in the same way. Steam the dumplings over boiling water for 15 minutes, until very glossy and cooked through. Test one dumpling to make sure the filling is cooked. While the dumplings are cooking, prepare the dipping sauces: place the garlic, ginger, scallion, and sherry in four separate dishes, and top up with the soy sauce. Serve the dim sum freshly cooked, garnished with scallion curls.

Dumplings with Gorgonzola – ITALY

INGREDIENTS

⅔ QUANTITY POTATO GNOCCHI
  (SEE RECIPE)

PINCH OF SALT

GENEROUS ¾ CUP MILK

4 TABLESPOONS BUTTER

4 OUNCES GORGONZOLA CHEESE,
  CRUMBLED INTO TINY PIECES

2 TABLESPOONS FRESHLY GRATED
  PARMESAN CHEESE

4 TABLESPOONS HEAVY CREAM

FOR THE GNOCCHI

1½ POUNDS BOILING – NOT BABY
  POTATOES

1 CUP BREAD FLOUR

PINCH OF SALT

serves 4 to 6

METHOD

Boil the gnocchi as you would pasta. But watch as they will cook more quickly – 3 to 4 minutes should be quite sufficient. As the gnocchi are cooking, heat the milk in a pan large enough to hold all the ingredients, including the gnocchi. As soon as the milk is warm, reduce the heat to a low simmer. Add the butter, the crumbled Gorgonzola, and the Parmesan. Slowly beat everything into a creamy paste. Remove from the heat. As soon as the pasta is cooked, drain it and add it to the sauce. Over a very low heat, stir in the cream. Serve this luxury number instantly.

To make potato gnocchi

Boil the potatoes in their skins until they are just soft. Peel them as soon as you can, and blend – or mash – them while still warm. Work in the flour, sifted with a little salt, until you have a pliable, sticky dough. Chop the dough into thumb-sized pieces. Press each one gently with a floured fork to flatten and serrate it.

Glossy dumplings ▶

Shrimp and Pork Dim Sum – CHINA

INGREDIENTS

1 CUP SHELLED, COOKED SHRIMP,
   GROUND

¾ CUP GROUND PORK

2 SCALLIONS, FINELY CHOPPED

1 TEASPOON SESAME OIL

1 GARLIC CLOVE, CRUSHED

2 TEASPOONS SOY SAUCE

1 EGG, BEATEN

SOY SAUCE, TO SERVE

FOR THE WON TON DOUGH

1½ CUPS ALL-PURPOSE FLOUR

½ CUP CORNSTARCH

PINCH OF SALT

1 EGG, BEATEN

½ CUP WATER

serves 12

METHOD

The shrimp may be finely chopped in a blender or food processor. Mix them with the pork, scallions, sesame oil, garlic, and soy sauce. Pound the mixture well so that all the ingredients bind together. Wet your hands, and shape the mixture into twenty-five small balls. Sift the flour, cornstarch and salt into a bowl, then make a well in the center. Add the egg, and pour in the water. Use a spoon to mix the egg and water in the flour. When the mixture binds together, scrape the spoon clean, and use your hands to work the dough into a small ball, leaving the bowl free of mixture. Knead the dough on a smooth surface until it is very smooth, and cover with plastic wrap. Chill for 15 to 30 minutes. Roll out the won ton dough into a 12½-inch square. Dust the surface with cornstarch as necessary to prevent the dough from sticking. Cut the dough into 5 2½-inch strips, then cut them across into squares. Brush a square of dough with a little beaten egg. Hold the dough on the palm of your hand, and place a shrimp ball on it. Flatten the shrimp ball slightly, and bring the dough up and around it, leaving the top of the mixture uncovered. Brush the dough with a little extra egg, if necessary, so that the folds cling to the side of the mixture. Shape the remaining dim sum in the same way – they should have flattened bases, and the dough should be wrinkled around their sides. Place the dim sum on a greased shallow dish which will fit in a steamer, then steam them over rapidly boiling water for 15 minutes, or until the shrimp mixture is cooked. While the dim sum are cooking, prepare small dishes of soy sauce. Serve the dim sum freshly cooked – they may be dipped into the soy sauce before eating.

Jamaican Grilled Lobster – CARIBBEAN

METHOD

Split each lobster in half, leaving the head and small claws on. Remove the meat from the head and tail, and discard the intestine, stomach and gills. Crack the claws carefully, and extract the meat. Cut the lobster meat into bite-sized pieces, and brush the outsides of the shells with a little oil, to keep them shiny. Shortly before serving, melt ¼ cup of the butter over a low heat with the garlic, and add the lobster meat, mixed herbs, cayenne pepper, and scallions, and a little salt and pepper. Heat the lobster meat through gently, for 2 to 3 minutes, shaking the pan occasionally. Pile back into the shells, and top with the parsley and bread crumbs. Dot with the remaining butter and cook under a hot, preheated broiler for 5 to 7 minutes, until the topping is crisp and golden. Serve immediately, accompanied by rum punch, lager or beer.

INGREDIENTS

2 COOKED LOBSTERS (BEST WHEN HEAVY FOR THEIR SIZE), WEIGHING ABOUT 1½ POUNDS EACH
A LITTLE OIL
⅓ CUP BUTTER
2 GARLIC CLOVES, CRUSHED
2 TEASPOONS MIXED FRESH HERBS OR 1 TEASPOON DRIED MIXED HERBS
2 PINCHES OF CAYENNE PEPPER
2 TABLESPOONS FINELY CHOPPED SCALLIONS
2 TABLESPOONS CHOPPED FRESH PARSLEY
3 TABLESPOONS FRESH WHITE BREAD CRUMBS
SALT AND FRESHLY GROUND BLACK PEPPER

serves 4

Dumplings with Chicken Livers – ITALY

METHOD

Cook the gnocchi by sifting the flour into the potatoes until you have a pliable, sticky dough. Cut the dough into small pieces. Press each piece with a floured fork to flatten and serrate it. Heat the oil in a skillet, and add the whole cloves of garlic and the onion. Soften in the oil until the onions begin to brown. Add the sage and the red wine; reduce the volume of the wine by half over a high heat. Remove. When all the gnocchi are ready, bring the red wine mixture back to a boil, and toss in the chicken livers. Cook for a minute or so, then add the cream. Bring the pan back to a boil, check the seasoning and take off the heat. Gently stir in the gnocchi. Serve immediately.

INGREDIENTS

1 POUND POTATOES
1 CUP ALL-PURPOSE FLOUR
PINCH OF SALT
2 TABLESPOONS OLIVE OIL
2 GARLIC CLOVES
1 SMALL ONION, VERY FINELY CHOPPED
1 TABLESPOON FINELY CHOPPED FRESH SAGE
⅔ CUP RED WINE
8 OUNCES CHICKEN LIVERS, VERY FINELY CHOPPED
⅔ CUP HEAVY CREAM

serves 4 to 6

Mushroom Dim Sum – CHINA

These are an excellent vegetarian alternative to the usual dim sum filled with pork or shrimp.

INGREDIENTS

4 LARGE CHINESE DRIED MUSHROOMS

4 CHINESE CABBAGE LEAVES

½ x 7-OUNCE CAN WATER CHESTNUTS,
  DRAINED AND CHOPPED

4 SCALLIONS, CHOPPED

1⅓ CUPS FINELY CHOPPED BUTTON
  MUSHROOMS

1 GARLIC CLOVE, CRUSHED

2 TABLESPOONS CORNSTARCH

PINCH OF SALT

1 EGG, BEATEN

1 QUANTITY WON TON DOUGH
  (PAGE 112)

FOR THE SAUCE

1 TABLESPOON OIL

1 TEASPOON SESAME OIL

2 SCALLIONS, CHOPPED

½ OUNCE PEELED AND FINELY
  SHREDDED, FRESH GINGER ROOT

1 CELERY STALK, CUT INTO FINE
  1-INCH STRIPS

1 CARROT, CUT INTO FINE 1-INCH STRIPS

2 TEASPOONS CORNSTARCH

2 TABLESPOONS SOY SAUCE

serves 25

METHOD

Place the mushrooms in a mug or very small bowl. Add just enough boiling water to cover them, then put a small saucer over them, and weight it down to keep the mushrooms submerged. Let stand for 20 minutes. Blanch the Chinese cabbage leaves in boiling water for 30 seconds, so they are just limp. Drain and squeeze all the water from them, then chop them finely. Drain the mushrooms, reserving the soaking liquid in a measuring cup and squeezing the water from the mushrooms. Discard any woody stalks, then chop the mushroom caps, and mix them with the Chinese cabbage leaves. Add the water chestnuts, scallions, button mushrooms, and garlic. Stir in the cornstarch and salt to taste. Add a little beaten egg to bind the mixture, so that it clumps easily. Prepare a large platter for the dim sum, and dust it with cornstarch. Cut the won ton dough in half. Roll out one portion into a 15-inch square, keeping the surface lightly dusted with cornstarch. Cut the dough into 5 x 3-inch strips, then across into squares. Brush a square of dough with beaten egg, then place a little of the mushroom mixture on it. Gather the dough up around the filling to make a small bundle. Press the dough together at the top to seal in the filling. Fill all the squares of

dough in the same way; then roll out the second half and repeat the process. Place the dim sum on the floured platter, and cover loosely with plastic wrap while you fill the remainder. For the sauce, heat the oil and sesame oil together in a small saucepan. Add the scallions, ginger, celery, and carrot. Stir-fry for 2 minutes. Measure the soaking liquid from the mushrooms, and add enough sherry to make it up to 1¼ cups. Blend the cornstarch to a smooth, thin paste with a little of the liquid, then stir in the rest of the liquid. Pour this into the pan, add the soy sauce, and bring to a boil, stirring. Reduce the heat ,and taste for seasoning. Let simmer very gently. Bring a large saucepan of salted water to the boil. Add the dim sum, bring back to a boil, and cook for 5 minutes. Do not boil the water rapidly. Drain well and place in a warmed serving dish. Ladle the sauce over the dim sum and serve.

Cook's Tip

The dim sum cook very well by steaming, but this does require a lot of steamer space. Several layers of bamboo steamer, placed on a wok, are ideal, and the dim sum should be placed in greased shallow dishes or on plates. If the plates are not greased, the dim sum will stick.

Tarte Marie-Odile – FRANCE

INGREDIENTS

1½ CUPS ALL-PURPOSE FLOUR

PINCH OF SALT

1 TEASPOON PAPRIKA

2 PINCHES OF CAYENNE PEPPER

½ CUP SOFTENED BUTTER

1 TABLESPOON GRATED PARMESAN
  CHEESE

1 EGG YOLK

4 CUPS RATATOUILLE

3 TABLESPOONS SOUR CREAM

⅓ CUP BLACK OLIVES

1 TABLESPOON COARSELY CHOPPED
  PARSLEY

serves 4 to 6

METHOD

Preheat the oven to 400°F. Sift together the flour, salt, paprika, and cayenne pepper. Rub in the softened butter until the mixture resembles fine bread crumbs. Add the Parmesan and egg yolk, and, if the dough seems too stiff and crumbly, add a little cold water. Press the dough into a shallow cake pan or a 9-inch quiche pan. Cover with foil and baking beans, and bake for about 20 minutes. Remove the foil, and return the

tart to the oven for 5 minutes longer to brown. While still warm, remove the pastry shell from its pan, and put it on a wire rack to cool. Place the pastry shell on a pretty plate, and fill with the chilled, drained ratatouille. Pour over the cream in a spiral, garnish with the olives, and sprinkle with the parsley. Serve immediately, or the pastry will lose its crispness.

Stuffed Pyzy – POLAND

Pyzy are made from raw potato, bound with cooked potato. They take slightly longer to cook than the other dumplings, but have a different flavor and texture that warrants the method. This recipe uses a cooked meat filling – a raw meat filling may be used, but the dumplings would take even longer to cook, and there is a danger of the potato mixture disintegrating. You may use other fillings equally successfully.

METHOD

Boil one potato in its skin until tender – about 20 minutes. Drain, cool, then peel. Rub the potato through a strainer. Peel and grate the second potato. Rinse it and squeeze all the water from the shreds. Mix the cooked and uncooked potato with the flour, ½ teaspoon salt and some pepper. Beat the mixture well so that it combines to a soft dough. Mix the ingredients for the filling. Divide the potato mixture into eight. Flour your hands, take a portion of potato, and flatten it on the palm of your hand into a patty. Place an eighth of the filling on the patty, then mold the potato around it to enclose it completely. The outside of the dumpling should be smooth, and the mixture should feel firmly bound together. This can be achieved by gently molding. Shape the other dumplings in the same way. Bring a saucepan of water to simmering point. Cook the dumplings at a steady simmer for 5 to 7 minutes. The pyzy will rise to the surface when cooked. They should look slightly glossy and feel firm. If any of the shreds of potato begin to separate from the dumplings, they are overcooking and will disintegrate soon, so lift them out of the water immediately. While the dumplings are cooking, brown the bacon in the fat. Transfer the dumplings to a warmed serving dish, and top with the bacon and fat. Serve at once.

INGREDIENTS

2 POTATOES, TOTAL WEIGHT
  1 POUND
¼ CUP ALL-PURPOSE FLOUR
SALT AND FRESHLY GROUND
  BLACK PEPPER

FOR THE FILLING

¾ CUP GROUND COOKED MEAT
½ SMALL ONION, GRATED
2–3 TABLESPOONS GOOD STOCK OR
  GRAVY
4 OUNCES PORK FAT BACK OR 8 SLICES
  RINDLESS FATTY BACON, DICED
A LITTLE FAT OR BUTTER

serves 4

Haloumi with Grapes – MIDDLE EAST

INGREDIENTS

12 OUNCES HALOUMI CHEESE

4 TABLESPOONS OLIVE OIL

1 TABLESPOON DRIED OREGANO

1 TEASPOON FRESH THYME LEAVES

2 TABLESPOONS COARSELY CRUSHED
    CORIANDER SEEDS

FRESHLY GROUND BLACK PEPPER

2 CUPS SEEDLESS GREEN GRAPES

1 BUNCH WATERCRESS

2 SCALLIONS, CHOPPED

serves 4

Haloumi is a tough ewes' milk cheese of the Middle East, Turkey and Greece. Often served barbecued, the cheese forms a crisp crust on cooking, and the middle softens to a pleasing texture. Serve this appetizer piping hot – the sweet, crisp grapes contrast deliciously with the cheese.

METHOD

Cut the cheese into ½- to 1-inch cubes, and place in a bowl. Add the olive oil, oregano, thyme, coriander, and a good sprinkling of black pepper. Mix well, cover and set aside to marinate for at least an hour; the cheese may be left overnight in the refrigerator. Remove all stalks from the grapes, then wash and dry them. Trim the leaves off the watercress, and mix them with the scallions. Divide this salad between four serving plates. Drain the oil from the cheese into a large pan, and heat it until quite hot – olive oil overheats quickly so this does not take long over medium to high heat. Put the cheese into the pan and stir-fry it until golden brown. Add the grapes, and toss them with the cheese for a few seconds simply to warm them slightly. Spoon the halloumi and grapes on the prepared salads, and serve at once, with crusty bread to savor the cooking juices.

Tomato Mozzarella Kebabs – ITALY

INGREDIENTS

4 OUNCES DRIED ROTELLE (PINWHEELS)

DASH OF OLIVE OIL, PLUS EXTRA
    4 TABLESPOONS

2 GARLIC CLOVES, CRUSHED

SALT AND FRESHLY GROUND BLACK
    PEPPER

8–12 CHERRY TOMATOES

8 OUNCES MOZZARELLA CHEESE, CUT
    INTO 1-INCH CUBES

serves 4

These are excellent for a vegetarian barbecue. Serve the kebabs with plenty of hot, crusty garlic bread and salad.

METHOD

Bring a large saucepan of water to a boil, and add the rotelle with a dash of olive oil. Cook for about 10 minutes, stirring occasionally, until tender. Drain and rinse under cold running water. Drain again and set aside. In a small bowl, combine the olive oil, garlic, salt and pepper. Set aside. To make the kebabs, place one rotelle, a tomato, then a cube of mozzarella cheese onto kebab skewers until all the ingredients have been used. Arrange the skewers on a baking sheet, and brush liberally with the garlic olive oil mixture, turning the kebabs to coat evenly. Place the kebabs under a preheated broiler for 5 to 7 minutes, turning the skewers halfway through cooking, until browned. Serve immediately.

Cook's Tip

If using wooden skewers, soak them for at least 1 hour in water before threading on the kebab ingredients. This will help prevent them from burning during broiling.

Jewish Piroshki — ISRAEL

Piroshki are tiny pastries, originally from Russia, usually eaten with a clear meat or chicken broth, but also delicious on their own. With the tremendous exodus of Russian Jews to America and Israel in recent years, these are becoming increasingly popular; they make a delightful canapé or hors-d'oeuvre. Traditionally made with a yeast-based dough, a good flaky pastry or commercial puff pastry can be used. The filling can vary from meat to fish, to mushrooms, to cheese and spinach, or any combination you like. Piroshki can be made ahead and refrigerated. Reheat in a 350°F oven 5 to 7 minutes before serving.

INGREDIENTS

1 TABLESPOON DRY YEAST

1 TABLESPOON SUGAR

¼ CUP LUKEWARM WATER

3–3½ CUPS ALL-PURPOSE FLOUR

2 TEASPOONS SALT

1 CUP LUKEWARM MILK

½ CUP UNSALTED BUTTER, MELTED AND
     COOLED

2 LARGE EGGS, LIGHTLY BEATEN

VEGETABLE OIL FOR GREASING BOWL

1 EGG, BEATEN WITH A PINCH OF SALT
     AND SUGAR, TO GLAZE

FOR THE MEAT FILLING

1 TABLESPOON VEGETABLE OIL

1 MEDIUM ONION, FINELY CHOPPED

1½ CUPS GROUND BEEF OR VEAL

1 TEASPOON SALT

PINCH OF FRESHLY GROUND BLACK
     PEPPER

¼ TEASPOON DRIED THYME

¼ TEASPOON GRATED NUTMEG

1 EGG, LIGHTLY BEATEN

serves 15

METHOD

Prepare the dough. Combine the yeast with the sugar and lukewarm water in a small bowl. Let stand until the mixture begins to foam, 10 to 15 minutes. Mix 3 cups of the flour and salt in a large bowl, and make a well in the center. Add the foamy yeast mixture, lukewarm milk, melted and cooled butter, and beaten eggs. Stir the mixture until a soft dough begins to form. Transfer the dough to a lightly floured work surface, and knead gently, adding a little flour if necessary to keep the dough from sticking. The dough will become smooth and slightly elastic after 10 to 15 minutes kneading. Form the dough into a ball, and place in an oiled bowl. Cover with a clean dish towel, and leave in a warm place until dough doubles in bulk, 1 to 1½ hours. Punch the dough down, cover and refrigerate overnight. (If the dough is needed quickly, cover and let rise again in a warm place for about another hour.) Prepare the filling. Heat the oil in a medium skillet, over medium heat. Add the chopped onion, and cook until the onion is soft and begins to color, about 5 minutes. Add the ground beef or veal and cook, stirring occasionally, until the meat has lost its pink color and any liquid has evaporated, 5 to 7 minutes. Season with salt, pepper, thyme, and nutmeg, and remove from the heat to cool slightly. Mix in the beaten egg, transfer to a medium bowl and refrigerate, covered, until ready to use. (Filling can be prepared several hours ahead.) Lightly grease two large baking sheets (you will need to work in batches). Cut the dough into three or four pieces; work on one piece at a time, and keep the remaining dough refrigerated. On a lightly floured surface, roll out the dough about ⅛-inch thick. Using a 3-inch round cutter, cut out as many rounds as possible. Brush the edge of each round with a little egg glaze. Place one rounded teaspoonful of filling on each round, and fold to form a half-moon shape. Carefully press the edges together. Repeat by rerolling any scraps of dough. Place on the baking sheet, cover with a clean dish towel, and leave in a warm place to rise, 20 minutes. Preheat the oven to 400°F. Brush the top of each half-moon with a little egg glaze, and bake until golden brown and puffed, 15 to 20 minutes. Serve warm with a little sour cream or yogurt.

Garlic Mushrooms – SPAIN

METHOD

Melt the butter in a large pan. Add the mushrooms, and sweat gently, covered, for 5 minutes, shaking occasionally. Add the lemon juice, salt and pepper. Increase the heat, tossing the mushrooms well. Add the garlic, toss and cook for 2 minutes. Add the cilantro or parsley, and cook for 1 minute. Remove from the heat and serve.

INGREDIENTS

⅓ CUP BUTTER

1½ POUNDS MUSHROOMS,
    BUTTON OR CAP

DASH OF LEMON JUICE

SALT AND FRESHLY GROUND
    BLACK PEPPER

3 TEASPOONS CRUSHED GARLIC

1 TABLESPOON CHOPPED FRESH
    CILANTRO OR PARSLEY

serves 4

Pasta-topped Mushrooms – ITALY

This dish is delicious served cold with a crisp leafy salad or warm as an appetizer or an accompaniment. The topping can be made ahead and arranged on the mushrooms at the last minute.

METHOD

Bring a large saucepan of water to a boil, and add the stellette with a dash of olive oil. Cook for about 7 minutes, stirring occasionally, until tender. Drain and set aside. Cut the stalks out of the mushrooms and discard. Arrange the mushrooms, stalk-side up, on a baking sheet and set aside. To make the topping, melt the butter in a skillet and sauté the garlic for about 2 minutes. Add the diced peppers, and cook for 5 to 7 minutes longer. Stir in the crumbled blue cheese and season to taste. Add the parsley and stellette. Stir well. Top each mushroom with the pasta mixture, then place the baking sheet under a hot broiler for 2 to 5 minutes, or until the topping is lightly golden and the mushrooms are warmed through. Serve immediately.

INGREDIENTS

2 OUNCES DRIED SMALL STELLETTE
    (STARS)

DASH OF OLIVE OIL

4 LARGE FLAT MUSHROOMS

¼ CUP BUTTER

1 GARLIC CLOVE, CRUSHED

½ YELLOW BELL PEPPER, SEEDED AND
    FINELY DICED

½ ORANGE BELL PEPPER, SEEDED AND
    FINELY DICED

5 OUNCES BLUE CHEESE, SUCH AS
    STILTON OR DANISH BLUE, CRUMBLED

SALT AND FRESHLY GROUND
    BLACK PEPPER

2 TABLESPOONS CHOPPED FRESH
    PARSLEY

serves 4

Spicy Oriental Squid – THAILAND

When the pieces of squid are stir-fried, they curl to expose the diamond cuts. The choice of cooking oil is important to achieve a high temperature and satisfactory crisp results.

INGREDIENTS

12 SQUID, CLEANED

JUICE OF 1 LEMON

1 FRESH GREEN CHILI, SEEDED AND
   CHOPPED

¼ TEASPOON FIVE-SPICE POWDER

2 GARLIC CLOVES, CRUSHED

2 TEASPOONS SESAME OIL

4 TABLESPOONS GROUNDNUT OIL

1 RED BELL PEPPER, SEEDED AND DICED

4 SCALLIONS, THINLY SLICED

4 TABLESPOONS SOY SAUCE

serves 4

METHOD

The tentacles may be used or not as preferred. Slit the squid body sacs lengthways, then cut each into 2 to 3 pieces. Using a small, sharp pointed knife, score a zigzag pattern on the inside of the pieces of squid. Do not cut right through the squid – simply mark a trellis pattern in the flesh. Place the squid pieces in a bowl. Add the lemon juice, chili, five-spice powder, garlic, and sesame oil, and mix well to coat all the pieces in seasoning. Cover and let marinate for at least an hour – if possible leave the squid for 3 to 4 hours. Heat the groundnut oil until simmering, then stir-fry the squid until browned. The pieces should curl to expose the attractive diamond cuts. Use a slotted spoon to remove the pieces from the pan, and divide them between 4 serving plates. Pour off any excess oil from the pan, if necessary, leaving just enough to cook the vegetables. Stir-fry the bell pepper and scallions for 1 to 2 minutes; then sprinkle in the soy sauce, and stir for a few seconds. Spoon the vegetable mixture and juices over the squid, and serve at once.

Kopytka – POLAND

The unmistakable similarity between these potato dumplings and potato gnocchi reflects the Italian influence on Polish cooking. They may be served as an accompaniment or as a main dish.

INGREDIENTS

1 POUND POTATOES

1 CUP ALL-PURPOSE FLOUR

½ TEASPOON SALT

1 EGG

¼ CUP BUTTER

serves 4

METHOD

Boil the potatoes in their skins until tender – about 20 minutes. Drain, cool, then peel. Rub the potatoes through a fine strainer. Stir in the flour and salt. Mix in the egg to make a soft dough. Take small portions of the dough, slightly smaller than walnuts, and roll into smooth balls. Make a deep indentation in each ball using your index finger. Alternatively, the kopytka may be molded into slightly squarer shapes. Bring a saucepan of water to a boil, then reduce the heat so that it is bubbling gently. Add the kopytka, and keep the water just bubbling. Cook for 4 to 5 minutes, until the little dumplings are firm and cooked. Taste one to make sure that they do not taste of raw flour. Do not overcook the kopytka, or they will become soggy. Drain well and place in a warmed serving dish. Melt the butter, and pour it over the dumplings.

Seafarer's Strudel – ENGLAND

You can use bought strudel pastry or even filo pastry for this recipe, but making your own is much more fun.

METHOD

Preheat the oven to 375°F. To make the filling, cook the cod steaks with a little water in a covered pan for about 10 minutes, or until the flesh is firm and flakes easily. Drain and break into bite-sized pieces with a fork. Boil the carrots in plenty of lightly salted water for about 7 to 10 minutes or until tender. Drain, toss in the butter and parsley, and let cool. Soak the golden raisins in hot water for about an hour until they swell. Drain and combine with the fish, carrots, bell peppers (to give a bit of crunch), garlic, lemon juice, garam masala, sugar, and turmeric, and season with salt and pepper to taste. Cover and keep in the refrigerator until needed. To make the strudel pastry, sift the flour and salt together, and beat together the egg, half the oil and most of the water. Stir into the flour to make a soft dough, adding water if necessary. Transfer the dough onto a well-floured surface, and knead with your fingertips for at least 10 minutes or until elastic. Put the kneaded dough into a floured bowl, cover with a cloth and leave in a warm place for 15 minutes. On a well-floured surface, roll the pastry out as thinly as possible, and transfer it carefully to a large, well-floured cloth. Brush with the remaining oil, and let to rest for 15 minutes. Pulling gently from the edges, stretch the dough until it is paper-thin. Cut off the thickened edges, and brush the dough with two thirds of the garlic butter. Sprinkle over the bread crumbs, and lay the filling down one edge of the dough, leaving a couple of inches free at either end. Fold over and roll up the strudel. Slide it onto a well-greased baking sheet – you may need to bend the strudel into a horseshoe to get it on – and brush thoroughly with the remaining garlic butter. Bake for about 30 minutes, and serve, cut into thick, slanting slices.

INGREDIENTS

1 POUND COD STEAKS

12 OUNCES YOUNG CARROTS, CUT INTO 1-INCH SLICES

2 TABLESPOONS BUTTER

1 TABLESPOON CHOPPED FRESH PARSLEY

⅓ CUP GOLDEN RAISINS

1 RED OR YELLOW BELL PEPPER, SEEDED AND THINLY SLICED (OPTIONAL)

1–2 GARLIC CLOVES, CRUSHED

1 TABLESPOON LEMON JUICE

1 TEASPOON GARAM MASALA

½ TEASPOON SUGAR

1 TEASPOON TURMERIC

SALT AND FRESHLY GROUND BLACK PEPPER

2 CUPS ALL-PURPOSE FLOUR

¼ TEASPOON SALT

1 SMALL EGG

⅔ CUP TEPID WATER

1 TABLESPOON OIL

½ CUP WARMED GARLIC BUTTER

3 TABLESPOONS SOFT WHITE BREAD CRUMBS

serves 6

Spinach and Mussel Pot – SPAIN

METHOD

If using fresh spinach, pick it over and discard any stalks and large veins. Wash thoroughly. Note: It is only necessary to cook fresh spinach. Place the spinach in boiling salted water. Boil for 2 minutes. Remove and cool under the cold faucet. Squeeze to remove all moisture. Chop finely. Sweat the onion in the butter. Add the spinach, garlic, nutmeg, salt and black pepper. Add the white wine, and turn up the heat. Cook for 5 minutes, until the wine has almost evaporated. Add the stock, and bring to a boil. Stir and cook for 5 minutes. The consistency should be that of heavy cream; if it's too thin, continue cooking over heat, stirring. Add the mussels, and cover the pot. Cook until the mussels have opened, continuously shaking the pot. Remove from the heat, and taste for seasoning. Ground black pepper will highlight the spinach flavor. Pour into bowls, evenly distributing the mussels. Swirl a little cream over each, and serve.

INGREDIENTS

1 POUND SPINACH

1 ONION, CHOPPED

¼ CUP BUTTER

1 TEASPOON CRUSHED GARLIC

PINCH OF NUTMEG

SALT AND FRESHLY GROUND BLACK PEPPER

1 GLASS OF DRY WHITE WINE

3¾ CUPS CHICKEN STOCK

2 PINTS MUSSELS, CLEANED AND DEBEARDED

2 TABLESPOONS LIGHT CREAM

serves 4

Dilled Shrimp in Smoked Kingfish Blanket – CARIBBEAN

INGREDIENTS

2 TABLESPOONS LIME OR LEMON JUICE

½ TEASPOON SALT

1 TABLESPOON CHOPPED FRESH
   CILANTRO

5 TABLESPOONS OLIVE OIL

1 TABLESPOON CHOPPED FRESH DILL

WHITE GROUND PEPPER

24 COOKED SHRIMP, SHELLED AND
   DEVEINED

4 OUNCES SMOKED KINGFISH, THINLY
   SLICED AND CHILLED

FRESH DILL SPRIGS, TO GARNISH

CHERRY TOMATOES, TO GARNISH

serves 4 to 6

Almost any thinly sliced smoked fish can be substituted for the Caribbean kingfish – just make certain the skin and bones have been removed. Choose the plumpest shrimp, however, so that the treasure inside the "blanket" can be fully savored. A garnish of fresh dill and cherry tomatoes will add even more drama to the serving plate.

METHOD

Combine the lime or lemon juice, salt, cilantro, olive oil, dill, and pepper in a glass bowl. Add the shrimp, cover, and marinate for 2 hours. Cut each slice of fish lengthways into strips ¼ inch wide. Wind a fish strip around each shrimp and fasten with a toothpick. Garnish and serve.

Ceviche of Shrimp – SPAIN

INGREDIENTS

1 QUART SHRIMP

2½ CUPS WATER

2½ CUPS LIME JUICE

2 RED ONIONS, CHOPPED

2 TABLESPOONS SOY SAUCE

SALT AND FRESHLY GROUND
   BLACK PEPPER

2 CUCUMBERS, SEEDED, SKINNED,
   HALVED LENGTHWISE AND CUT INTO
   HALF MOONS

1 RED BELL PEPPER, SEEDED AND THINLY
   SLICED

1 BUNCH OF DILL, CHOPPED

TABASCO SAUCE, TO TASTE

LIME WEDGES, TO GARNISH

serves 4

METHOD

Place the shrimp in a large bowl. Mix the ingredients for the marinade together (water, lime juice, red onions, soy sauce, salt and pepper), and pour over the shrimp. Marinate for 20 minutes. Add the cucumber, bell pepper slices and dill. Toss. Spoon onto plates or into small bowls. Sprinkle with pepper and Tabasco sauce. Serve with lime wedges.

Dilled shrimp in smoked kingfish blanket ▶

Mussel Pancakes – SPAIN

Galician mussels are the best in the world, and this simple recipe shows them off perfectly. The thin crêpes are related to the ones made in Brittany, which shares the same Celtic culture. Sweet ones are made with milk and filled with custard for dessert. Savory crêpes may also be made with blood at pig-killing time.

INGREDIENTS

2 QUARTS MUSSELS

½ CUP DRY WHITE WINE

2 TABLESPOONS CHOPPED ONION

4 PARSLEY STALKS, BRUISED

6 BLACK PEPPERCORNS, CRUSHED

FOR THE CRÊPES

1 CUP LESS 2 TABLESPOONS ALL-
PURPOSE FLOUR

2 LARGE EGGS

MUSSEL LIQUOR (SEE METHOD)

4–6 TABLESPOONS THICK CREAM

ABOUT 4 TABLESPOONS BUTTER

6 TABLESPOONS CHOPPED FRESH
PARSLEY

serves 6

METHOD

Wash the mussels, discarding any that are open (and do not close when touched). Pull off the beards. Put the wine, onion, parsley stalks, and peppercorns in a big pan, and bring to a simmer. Put in the mussels (in two batches), and cover tightly. Cook over a high heat for 3 to 4 minutes shaking occasionally, until they are open. Discard the shells and any mussels that remain shut or smell strongly. Strain the liquid into a measuring jug, and let cool. Taste for seasoning. Make the crêpe batter. Put the flour in a bowl or blender, and work in the eggs, mussel liquor, and 2 tablespoons of cream. (Don't overbeat in a blender.) Let it stand, if you can, for an hour. Melt 1½ tablespoons of butter in a skillet, swirling it round. Add to the batter, and stir thoroughly. Heat another ½ tablespoon of butter and swirl.

Use about ¼ cup batter per crêpe: it is easiest to pour from a cup. Lift the pan and pour the batter fast into the middle of the pan and in a ring around, tilting the pan to cover the bottom. (If you overdo the liquid, spoon off anything that doesn't set at once: crêpes should be thin.) Put the pan back over the heat, shaking it to make sure the crêpe does not stick. Cook for a minute until golden underneath, then flip over with a fish slice (picking up with fingers is just as easy). Briefly fry the other side. Roll and keep warm on a plate while you make more. Warm the remaining cream in a saucepan with the mussel bodies. Spoon mussels and a little cream onto one edge of a pancake, sprinkle with parsley and roll up. Do not keep them waiting long.

Baked Avocado Crab – CARIBBEAN

INGREDIENTS

1 TABLESPOON BUTTER

2 TABLESPOONS ALL-PURPOSE FLOUR

¾ CUP HOT MILK

1 TEASPOON GRATED PARMESAN CHEESE

1 TEASPOON TOMATO PASTE

1¼ CUPS FLAKED CANNED OR FROZEN
CRAB MEAT

PINCH OF SALT AND DASH OF TABASCO
TO TASTE

2 RIPE AVOCADOS

serves 4

METHOD

Preheat the oven to 325°F. Melt the butter over a medium heat. Add the flour, and cook for a minute, taking care not to let it brown. Gradually stir in the hot milk, then let the sauce simmer for 4 minutes to cook the flour. Off the heat, add the Parmesan, tomato paste, and crab meat, and season to taste. Halve the avocados and discard the pits. Remove about 2 teaspoons of flesh from each half, mash finely and add to the crab

mixture. Pile this into the avocado halves, arrange them in a baking dish and cook in the oven until heated through and just beginning to brown, about 20 minutes. Serve immediately. If you are using fresh crab meat, simmer the shell in a little water and white wine, and use some of this stock to replace half the milk when making the sauce.

Jewish-style Curried Fish Fillets – INDIA

This dish comes from one of the Jewish communities in India, the southern city of Cochin. Cochin is near the Kerala Coast which produces fresh fish and is also famous for its spice market. This is best served with rice.

METHOD

Heat the oil in a large skillet, over a medium-high heat. Add the sliced onion, and cook until softened and beginning to color, 3 to 5 minutes. Add the garlic, and cook for 1 minute longer. Add the fish, and cook until it begins to firm and turn opaque, 4 to 5 minutes. Gently stir in the remaining ingredients, except the garnish and rice, and ½ cup water, and simmer for 15 minutes, covered. The fish will flake easily if tested with the tip of a knife. Remove the fish fillets to a serving dish. Increase the heat to high, and cook the sauce until slightly thickened, 2 to 3 minutes. Pour over the fish fillets. Garnish with cilantro, and serve with hot rice.

INGREDIENTS

1 TABLESPOON VEGETABLE OIL

1 ONION, CUT IN HALF AND THINLY SLICED

2–3 GARLIC CLOVES, PEELED AND FINELY CHOPPED

2 POUNDS WHITE FISH FILLETS, SUCH AS COD, HALIBUT OR WHITING, CUT IN 3-INCH PIECES

¼ CUP FRESH CHOPPED CILANTRO

1 TABLESPOON WHITE OR RED WINE VINEGAR

4 TABLESPOONS TOMATO PASTE

1 TEASPOON GROUND CUMIN

½ TEASPOON TURMERIC

1 SMALL FRESH RED CHILI, OR ½ TEASPOON DRIED RED PEPPER FLAKES

FRESH CILANTRO, TO GARNISH

serves 6

Nutty Ricky Ricardo Chicken – AMERICA

These are great to serve with cocktails since the guests do not have to deal with a messy dipping sauce.

INGREDIENTS

12 CHICKEN WINGS OR
   CHICKEN WING DRUMETTES
SALT AND FRESHLY GROUND
   BLACK PEPPER
2 TABLESPOONS CREAMY PEANUT BUTTER
2 TABLESPOONS SOY SAUCE
1½ TABLESPOONS HONEY
½ TEASPOON GROUND CUMIN
1 GARLIC CLOVE, MINCED
¼–½ TEASPOON DRIED HOT RED PEPPER
   FLAKES TO TASTE, OR ½ FRESH OR
   CANNED JALAPEÑO CHILI, SEEDED
   AND FINELY MINCED
¾ CUP FINELY CHOPPED SALTED OR
   UNSALTED ROASTED PEANUTS
3–4 TABLESPOONS FINELY CHOPPED
   FRESH CILANTRO

serves 4

METHOD

Preheat the oven to 400°F. In a shallow baking sheet lined with foil, season the chicken wings or drumettes with salt and pepper. Bake in the middle of the oven for 30 minutes, or until they begin to turn brown and become crisp. While the chicken wings are baking, stir together the peanut butter, soy sauce, honey, cumin, garlic, and pepper flakes in a small saucepan. Cook over a low heat, stirring until smooth. Brush the chicken wings generously with the sauce and bake them for 10 to 15 minutes longer. Sprinkle the chicken wings immediately with the chopped peanuts and cilantro and let them cool slightly before serving.

Roasted Spareribs with Lemon Grass and Chili – VIETNAM

INGREDIENTS

12 PORK SPARERIBS
2 TABLESPOONS CLEAR HONEY
1 TEASPOON FIVE-SPICE POWDER
2 GARLIC CLOVES, FINELY CHOPPED AND
   CRUSHED
3 TABLESPOONS DRY SHERRY OR RICE
   WINE
3 TABLESPOONS NUOC MAM SAUCE OR
3 TABLESPOONS LIGHT SOY SAUCE MIXED
   WITH 1 TEASPOON ANCHOVY SAUCE
2 STALKS FRESH LEMON GRASS, SLICED
   THINLY, OR GRATED RIND OF 1
   LEMON
2 FRESH RED CHILIES, FINELY CHOPPED

serves 4

METHOD

Wash and dry the spareribs, and place them in a large bowl. In another bowl, combine the honey, five-spice powder, garlic, dry sherry, Nuoc Mam, lemon grass, and chili. Mix well. Spread the honey mixture over the spare ribs, and let marinate for 4 hours. The ribs can be cooked over a barbecue, turning frequently and basting with the marinade; or baked in a preheated oven at 375°F, basting with the marinade; or broiled under a moderately hot broiler, basting with the marinade.

Trinidad-style Cilantro Chicken – CARIBBEAN

METHOD

Season the chicken with the salt, pepper, garlic, lemon juice, and half the ground coriander. Chop the fresh cilantro finely, and mix it in with the chicken, then let marinate for 4 hours. Preheat the oven to 350°F. Drain the chicken. Melt the butter or margarine. Place the chicken in a heatproof dish, and pour the melted butter or margarine over the chicken. Sprinkle with the remaining ground coriander, then bake for 1 hour, or until the chicken is cooked. Just before serving, broil the chicken to brown it. Serve with rice and salad.

INGREDIENTS

3-POUND CHICKEN, CUT INTO
   2-INCH PIECES

1 TEASPOON SALT

½ TEASPOON FRESHLY GROUND BLACK
   PEPPER

3 GARLIC CLOVES

2 TEASPOONS LEMON JUICE

2 TABLESPOONS GROUND CORIANDER

1 SMALL BUNCH FRESH CILANTRO

3 TABLESPOONS BUTTER OR MARGARINE

serves 4

Chicken Empanada – SPAIN

METHOD

Preheat the oven to 400°F. Heat the oil. Slowly cook the onion and bacon in it. Add the garlic, green bell pepper, chilies, paprika, sliced mushrooms, and raisins if used. Stir and add the parsley and soy sauce. Pour on the wine and stock, stir, and simmer for 20 minutes. In a separate pan, melt the butter, and add the chicken cubes. Toss until browned all over, and add to the vegetables. Stir and simmer for 5 minutes. Remove from the heat. Heat the oil in a skillet and slowly cook the onion and garlic.

Add the bell pepper and chilies, and cook for 10 minutes. Stir in the stock, cover and cook for 20 minutes. Grease and line a paella pan with half the dough and add the filling. Let stand for 10 minutes, then bake for 30 minutes.

Cook's Tip

If you wish to make individual empanadas, cut out 6-inch rounds of pastry. Place the filling in one half and cover with the remaining dough, sealing well.

INGREDIENTS

475 G/18 OZ YEAST DOUGH

¼ CUP BUTTER

FOR THE FILLING

4 TABLESPOONS OLIVE OIL

1 ONION, CHOPPED

1½ CUPS CHOPPED FATTY BACON

3 TEASPOONS CRUSHED GARLIC

1 GREEN BELL PEPPER, SEEDED AND
   SLICED

2 CHILIES, SEEDED AND CHOPPED

1 TEASPOON PAPRIKA

2 CUPS SLICED BUTTON MUSHROOMS

½ CUP RAISINS (OPTIONAL)

2 TEASPOONS CHOPPED FRESH PARSLEY

2 TEASPOONS SOY SAUCE

1 GLASS OF DRY WHITE WINE

1¼ CUPS CHICKEN STOCK

2 TABLESPOONS BUTTER

6 CUPS BONELESS CUBED CHICKEN MEAT

serves 2

Shrimp and Ground Pork on Sugar Cane – VIETNAM

INGREDIENTS

1 TABLESPOON DRIED SHRIMP
  (OPTIONAL)
1 CUP SHELLED SHRIMP
GENEROUS 1 CUP GROUND PORK
1 SMALL ONION, FINELY CHOPPED
2 TABLESPOONS FINELY CHOPPED FRESH
  CILANTRO
SALT AND FRESHLY GROUND
  BLACK PEPPER
1 TABLESPOON NUOC MAM SAUCE OR
1 TABLESPOON LIGHT SOY SAUCE MIXED
  WITH ½ TEASPOON ANCHOVY SAUCE
1 EGG, BEATEN
4 X 6-INCH LENGTHS OF SUGAR CANE
  OR BAMBOO SKEWERS
ALL-PURPOSE FLOUR OR CORNSTARCH
  (OPTIONAL)
VEGETABLE OIL FOR DEEP-FRYING
  (OPTIONAL)

serves 4

METHOD

If using dried shrimp, soak for about 1 hour in warm water. Squeeze out excess water, and chop finely. Wash the fresh shrimp and chop finely. Put the ground pork into a large bowl. Add the onion, cilantro, fresh and dried shrimp, salt and pepper, and Nuoc Mam sauce. Pour the egg into the pork and shrimp mixture, and mix well with your hand. The mixture should come together so that it can be molded around the lengths of sugar cane or around bamboo skewers. If it is too runny, sift a little all-purpose flour or cornstarch into the mixture. Peel the sugar cane, leaving 1 inch of the green covering on at each end, or 2 inches at one end. Mold the mixture onto the peeled part of the sugar cane. Broil the sticks under a medium hot broiler, turning to make sure they cook evenly. Make sure that the sugar cane does not burn. Alternatively, deep-fry in hot oil for 4 to 6 minutes. Serve on a bed of lettuce. The sugar cane should be chewed or sucked as you eat the shrimp and pork.

Meatballs in Tomato Sauce – GREECE

INGREDIENTS

6 CUPS GROUND LAMB

2 SLICES BROWN BREAD

4 TABLESPOONS MILK

1 TABLESPOON OLIVE OIL

1 ONION, CHOPPED

1 TOMATO, PEELED, SEEDED AND CHOPPED

¾ CUP LONG-GRAIN RICE

1 TABLESPOON CHOPPED FRESH MINT

PINCH OF GROUND CINNAMON

2 TABLESPOONS CHOPPED FRESH PARSLEY

1 EGG, BEATEN

¼ CUP RED WINE

SALT AND FRESHLY GROUND BLACK PEPPER

5 CUPS WATER

4 TABLESPOONS TOMATO PASTE

1 GARLIC CLOVE, CRUSHED

CHOPPED FRESH PARSLEY, TO GARNISH

serves 6 to 8

This rich, tasty dish can be made well and kept in the refrigerator – in fact, it tastes better reheated the next day.

METHOD

Place the ground lamb in a large mixing bowl. Remove the crusts from the bread, and place the bread on a plate. Sprinkle over the milk, and let soak for 10 minutes, or until all the milk has been soaked up into the bread. Add the bread to the mixing bowl. Using your hand, mix the meat and bread together thoroughly. Heat the olive oil in a small saucepan, and sauté the onion and chopped tomato flesh for about 5 minutes. Add to the mixing bowl with the rice, mint, cinnamon, parsley, beaten egg, wine, and salt and pepper. Mix well to combine all the ingredients. Place the water in a large, deep skillet, and stir in the tomato paste. Add the garlic, and heat slowly to bring to a boil. Simmer for 5 minutes. Using slightly damp hands, shape the meat mixture into round balls, about the size of a golf ball, and carefully place them in the simmering tomato sauce. Cover the skillet, and cook for about 30 minutes, or until the rice is cooked and the sauce has thickened. Serve garnished with chopped parsley.

Jamaican Baked Papaya with Meat Filling – CARIBBEAN

INGREDIENTS

2 TABLESPOONS VEGETABLE OIL

1 SMALL ONION, FINELY CHOPPED

1 GARLIC CLOVE, CRUSHED

4 CUPS LEAN GROUND BEEF OR LAMB

4 RIPE TOMATOES, PEELED AND CHOPPED

2 FRESH CHILIES, THINLY CHOPPED FOR
    A MILD FLAVOR

SALT AND FRESHLY GROUND
    BLACK PEPPER

5 POUNDS GREEN PAPAYAS, HALVED AND
    SEEDED

¼ CUP GRATED CHEESE

serves 6

METHOD

Preheat the oven to 350°F. Heat the oil in a large skillet, and fry the onion and garlic in it for 5 minutes. Then, stir in the beef or lamb, and cook until browned. Add the tomatoes, chili, salt and freshly ground black pepper to taste. Continue to cook until all the liquid has evaporated. Spoon the meat mixture into the papaya shells, and place them in a shallow roasting pan. Pour inenough boiling water around them to come about 1 inch up the sides of the shells when they are placed side by side. Bake for 1 hour. Sprinkle with half the grated cheese, and bake for 30 minutes longer. Serve sprinkled with the remaining grated cheese.

Snail Rolls – FRANCE

INGREDIENTS

4 LARGE SOFT WHITE ROLLS

3–4 GARLIC CLOVES, CRUSHED

½ CUP SOFTENED BUTTER

1 TABLESPOON CHOPPED SCALLIONS

1 TABLESPOON CHOPPED FRESH PARSLEY

SALT AND FRESHLY GROUND
    BLACK PEPPER

16 CANNED SNAILS WITH SHELLS

serves 4

METHOD

Preheat the oven to 425°F. Cut the top third off each roll, and scoop out four depressions, each large enough to hold a snail shell. Mash the garlic with the softened butter, scallions, and parsley, and season with a little salt and pepper. Drain the snails, and put each into its shell. Fill the shells with the garlic and butter mixture. Put four stuffed snail shells into each bun, keepingthem as upright as possible. Arrange them on a baking sheet, and cook for about 7 minutes, or until the butter has melted and the snails are heated through. Cover with the roll tops, and lower the temperature to 350°F, while you seat your guests, and serve.

Chicken Livers with Sherry Vinegar – SPAIN

INGREDIENTS

1 TEASPOON PAPRIKA

1 TEASPOON GARLIC

½ TEASPOON SALT

½ TEASPOON FRESHLY GROUND BLACK
    PEPPER

1 POUND CHICKEN LIVERS, TRIMMED (TO
    REMOVE ANY GRISTLE AND THE GREEN
    BILE SACS) AND WASHED

¼ CUP MELTED BUTTER

½ ONION, FINELY CHOPPED

¼ CUP SHERRY VINEGAR

1 TEASPOON SUGAR

1¼ CUPS CHICKEN STOCK

serves 4

METHOD

Mix the paprika, garlic, salt and pepper together in a bowl. Toss the livers in, mixing the seasoning well over them. Heat a large skillet, add the melted butter and get it hot. Add the livers to the pan, stirring immediately over a high heat. Keep tossing to seal the livers and brown all over. Remove the livers to a warmed bowl. Add the onion to the pan, and soften over a lower heat. Turn up the heat again, add the vinegar and sugar. Cook until the vinegar has almost evaporated. Add the stock, stir and reduce to half the quantity. Break the remaining butter into small pieces, and shake into the pan until it is all absorbed. Check the seasoning and pour over the livers, either in one large bowl or several

Mini Kebabs – GREECE

Souvlakia is the Greek word for small pieces of meat (and in some cases vegetables too) threaded onto skewers and cooked over a barbecue. In this recipe the kebabs are cooked in the oven, although you could certainly use the barbecue if you wish.

METHOD

Preheat the oven to 375°F. Cut the lamb into 1-inch cubes, and place in a large shallow dish. Combine all the remaining ingredients together in a screw-top jar, and shake well. Pour the marinade evenly over the meat, and stir to coat. Cover and let marinate in a cool place for several hours or overnight. Thread the cubes of meat onto skewers, and place the kebabs on baking sheets. Bake for 15 to 20 minutes, turning occasionally, until browned and cooked through. Serve the kebabs on the skewers with pocket bread and plenty of green salad on the *meze* table.

INGREDIENTS

2 POUNDS BONELESS LEG OF LAMB

½ CUP OLIVE OIL

1 TEASPOON GROUND CUMIN

1 TEASPOON DRIED OREGANO

2 BAY LEAVES, CRUSHED

2 GARLIC CLOVES, CRUSHED

1 ONION, VERY FINELY CHOPPED

¼ CUP RED WINE

¼ CUP RED WINE VINEGAR

2 TABLESPOONS LEMON JUICE

SALT AND FRESHLY GROUND
   BLACK PEPPER

serves 6 to 8

Soups

~

Beet Borscht – POLAND

There are many versions of borscht; the only ingredient which does not vary are the beets! This soup is made all over Eastern Europe, and served hot or cold. It can be made with beef or without, with vegetables or without, and served chunky or smooth. This elegant ruby-red purée is most delicious served with a swirl of sour cream, snipped chives and dill.

INGREDIENTS

1½ POUNDS SMALL BEETS WITH TOPS

1 ONION, CHOPPED

3¾ CUPS BEEF, CHICKEN OR
    VEGETABLE STOCK, OR WATER

1 TEASPOON SALT

FRESHLY GROUND BLACK PEPPER

3 TABLESPOONS LEMON JUICE OR CIDER
    VINEGAR

2 TABLESPOONS LIGHT BROWN SUGAR,
    OR TO TASTE

SOUR CREAM FOR SERVING

SNIPPED FRESH CHIVES AND DILL, TO
    GARNISH

serves 6

METHOD

Cut the tops from the beets, leaving 2 to 3 inches of stalk attached. Scrub the beets thoroughly under cold running water, being sure to remove all grit and sand. If the tops are young and tender, they may be added, well washed. In a large saucepan, over medium heat, place the beets and chopped onion, and cover with stock or water. Bring to a boil, then simmer, partially covered, until the beets are tender, 20 to 30 minutes. Carefully strain the liquid through a strainer into a large heatproof bowl; rinse the saucepan. Remove the beets, and peel off the skin. Quarter the beets, and add to a blender or food processor. Add the onions (and tops if using) from the strainer to the beets; process until finely puréed. Return the beet and onion purée to the washed saucepan, and add the reserved cooking liquid, being careful not to add any sand or grit which may have settled on bottom. Bring the soup to a boil over a medium heat. Season with salt, pepper, lemon juice or vinegar, and brown sugar. Simmer for 5 minutes, and serve hot with a swirl of sour cream. Sprinkle with fresh chives and dill. Alternatively, cool and chill to serve cold.

Fragrant Lettuce Soup – ENGLAND

INGREDIENTS

6 GARLIC CLOVES, UNPEELED

2 LARGE CABBAGE-TYPE LETTUCES

3 TABLESPOONS FINELY CHOPPED ONION

3 TABLESPOONS BUTTER

4 TABLESPOONS FLOUR

½ TEASPOON SUGAR

SALT AND FRESHLY GROUND
    BLACK PEPPER

3¾ CUPS MILK OR MILK AND WATER,
    MIXED

2 EGG YOLKS

3 TABLESPOONS LIGHT CREAM

1 TABLESPOON CHOPPED FRESH PARSLEY,
    CHIVES OR MINT, TO GARNISH

serves 4

METHOD

Plunge the unpeeled garlic cloves into boiling water, and simmer for 8 minutes. Drain, peel and chop them coarsely. Wash the lettuce, and shred it finely. Stew it gently with the onions in the butter for 5 minutes. Stir in the parboiled garlic and cook for 5 minutes longer. Remove from the heat, and add the flour, sugar, and a little salt and pepper. Return to the heat, and add the milk. Bring to a boil, and simmer for 15 minutes, or until the vegetables are tender. Either strain or blend the soup, and return it to the saucepan.

Check the seasoning. Combine the egg yolks and cream, stir them into the soup, and heat to just below boiling point (if boiled, the egg yolks will get stringy). Sprinkle the chopped fresh parsley, chives or mint over each bowlful.

Variation

For a more intense flavor, add a handful of coarsely chopped watercress leaves to the stewing lettuce.

Beet borscht ▶

Shchav – RUSSIAN FEDERATION

This is a Russian soup made from sorrel, also called "sour grass," which is generally served cold. Sorrel can be difficult to find unless you are lucky enough to grow it in your garden, but young spinach leaves make a good substitute, although they lack the sharpness of the sorrel leaves. This soup was frequently served on Shavuot.

INGREDIENTS

1 POUND SORREL OR YOUNG SPINACH
    LEAVES, WELL RINSED AND COARSELY
    CHOPPED

1 BUNCH WATERCRESS, CHOPPED

1 ONION, CHOPPED

1 CELERY STALK, FINELY CHOPPED

2 QUARTS VEGETABLE STOCK (OPTIONAL)

JUICE AND GRATED RIND OF 1 LEMON

2–3 TABLESPOONS SUGAR

PINCH OF SALT

FRESHLY GROUND BLACK PEPPER

SOUR CREAM AND FRESH DILL SPRIGS,
    TO GARNISH

serves 4

METHOD

Place the sorrel or spinach, watercress, onion, and celery into a large casserole. Pour in the vegetable stock or water. Bring to a boil over a high heat, then simmer partially covered, 20 minutes, until the watercress is just tender. Cool slightly. Ladle the soup into a blender or food processor. Blend or process until finely puréed.

Return the soup to the pan, and add the lemon juice and rind, sugar, salt and pepper to taste. Pour into a nonmetallic container, and cool completely. Refrigerate for at least 3 to 4 hours or until ready to serve. Serve Shchav in chilled bowls, topped with a dollop of sour cream and sprig of dill.

Chicken Soup with Matzo Balls – ISRAEL

Chicken soup, also known as "Jewish penicillin," is thought by Jewish mothers to cure all ills! It is a simple soup made all over the world, and the seasonings used reflect its regional origins. Matzo balls are one of the most popular accompaniments, but noodles, rice, tiny matzo squares, flour-based dumplings (kreplach), can all be added.

INGREDIENTS

1 LARGE BOILING FOWL, ABOUT
    5 POUNDS QUARTERED (ASK THE
    BUTCHER TO INCLUDE GIBLETS, NECK
    AND FEET, BUT NOT LIVERS)

3 CARROTS, CUT INTO PIECES

2 MEDIUM ONIONS, A FEW SKINS
    RESERVED

3 LEEKS, SPLIT AND WELL RINSED

1 RIPE TOMATO, QUARTERED AND SEEDED

2 GARLIC CLOVES, PEELED

2 CHICKEN BOUILLON CUBES (OPTIONAL)

1 TABLESPOON BLACK PEPPERCORNS

1 TEASPOON SALT

STEMS FROM 1 SMALL BUNCH FRESH
    PARSLEY

FOR THE MATZO BALLS

1 CUP MEDIUM MATZO MEAL

½ TEASPOON SALT

½ TEASPOON FRESHLY GROUND BLACK
    PEPPER

¼ TEASPOON GROUND GINGER

¼ TEASPOON GROUND CINNAMON

1 CUP BOILING WATER

2 TABLESPOONS VERY FINELY GROUND,
    BLANCHED ALMONDS

2 TABLESPOONS CHICKEN FAT OR SOFT
    MARGARINE

1 EGG, LIGHTLY BEATEN

serves 8 to 10

METHOD

Remove any excess fat from the inside and outside of the chicken. Remove any yellow or green bits from the giblets. Place the chicken pieces, giblets, neck and feet in a large bowl. Pour over boiling water and drain. Scrape off any hard skin from the feet. Place the chicken pieces, neck and feet in a large stockpot, and cover with cold water. Over a high heat, bring to a boil, then skim off any foam which comes to the surface. Add the giblets and remaining soup ingredients, except parsley for garnish, and bring to a boil, skimming off any more foam which comes to the surface. Reduce the heat to low, and simmer for about 3 hours. Strain the soup into a large heatproof bowl, reserving the chicken pieces and giblets. Cool the soup, then refrigerate, covered, overnight. Remove the meat from the chicken bones, and cut into small pieces. Cut the giblets into small pieces, and add

to the chicken pieces. Refrigerate, covered, overnight. Prepare the matzo balls. Mix matzo meal with salt, pepper, ginger, and cinnamon in a large bowl. Pour the boiling water over and stir. Add the finely ground almonds, chicken fat or soft margarine, and beaten egg. Mix and refrigerate for at least 2 hours. To serve, remove the cold soup from the refrigerator, and carefully remove any congealed fat from the surface. Transfer to a large saucepan, add the cut-up chicken and giblets, and bring to a boil. Remove the matzo-ball mixture from the refrigerator. Scoop out the mixture, and form into 1-inch balls, rolling the mixture between wet palms of hands. Drop the balls into simmering soup, and cook until the matzo balls are floating and puffed, 20 to 30 minutes. Do not let the soup boil, or the balls will fall apart. Stir in the chopped fresh parsley, and serve immediately.

Butternut Squash Soup — AMERICA

INGREDIENTS

2 MEDIUM BUTTERNUT SQUASH
(APPROXIMATELY 3 POUNDS)

1–2 TABLESPOONS OLIVE OIL

3 TABLESPOONS BUTTER

2 LEEKS (ABOUT 1½ POUNDS) CHOPPED,
WHITE PART ONLY

3 CUPS CHICKEN STOCK

¼ TEASPOON WHITE PEPPER

½ TEASPOON DRIED OREGANO

½ TEASPOON DRIED THYME

1 CUP BUTTERMILK

PINCH OF SALT

serves 4 to 6

This is a versatile soup: it can be made with different kinds of squashes, including acorn and zucchini, so you can enjoy it throughout the year, changing it to fit whatever is in season. The buttermilk adds a creamy, slightly tangy flavor rather than a sharp, identifiable buttermilk taste, so you don't have to be a buttermilk-lover to like it. However, if you really dislike buttermilk, you can substitute heavy cream. To save time, bake the squash the night before you plan to eat the soup.

METHOD

Preheat the oven to 350°F. Cut the squash in half lengthways, and brush the flesh with olive oil. Bake until tender, about 45 minutes. Let cool slightly. Scoop out the pulp. Sauté the leeks in butter in a heavy saucepan for 10 minutes. Add the squash, stock, and seasonings. Bring to a boil, and simmer for 10 minutes. In batches, purée the soup in a blender or food processor. Return to the heat, and bring to a boil. Add the buttermilk and heat, but do not let the soup boil. Add salt to taste.

Chilled Salad Soup – KAZAKHSTAN

This is an extraordinarily refreshing soup – like a liquid salad. Based on ingredients found all over the Central Republics, it is a refined variation on a common theme.

INGREDIENTS

3 GARLIC CLOVES

4 THICK SLICES GREEK OR FRENCH
    BREAD, CRUSTS REMOVED

¼ CUP BUTTER

2 RED ONIONS, THINLY SLICED

8 RADISHES, THINLY SLICED

7 LARGE RIPE TOMATOES, PEELED,
    SEEDED AND CHOPPED

½ CUCUMBER, PEELED AND THINLY
    SLICED

SALT AND FRESHLY GROUND
    BLACK PEPPER

LARGE DASH OF TABASCO

5 TABLESPOONS VEGETABLE OIL

1 TABLESPOON LEMON JUICE

14-OUNCE CAN CHICKEN
    CONSOMMÉ

⅓ CUP GREEK- OR BULGARIAN-STYLE
    YOGURT

8 SCALLIONS, FINELY CHOPPED

serves 4 to 6

METHOD

Finely chop two of the garlic cloves, and set aside. Use the remaining clove to rub over the bread slices. Coarsely cut them into croûtons. Heat the butter in a skillet, and sauté the croûtons until golden. Drain and set aside. Combine the chopped garlic, red onions, radishes, tomatoes, cucumber, and seasoning to taste in a large bowl, and add the Tabasco. Whisk together the oil and lemon juice in a small bowl; then pour over the salad, and chill for 1 hour. Place the chicken consommé in the refrigerator 30 minutes before you make the soup. Just before serving, add the chilled consommé to the bowl, and stir it in thoroughly, then stir in the yogurt. Sprinkle with the scallions, and serve the croûtons in a separate bowl.

Aruban Chicken and Vegetable Soup – CARIBBEAN

METHOD

Cut the chicken into eight pieces, and put into a large saucepan with the stock. Bring to a boil over a high heat. Skim off the foam with a large spoon; then reduce the heat, partially cover, and simmer for 45 minutes. Skim the fat from the soup. Add the tomatoes, corn, yams, potatoes, pumpkin, peas, chilies, salt and freshly ground black pepper, and bring to a boil. Reduce the heat, and simmer for about 20 minutes, or until the chicken and vegetables are cooked. Taste the soup, adjusting the seasoning if necessary. Stir in the chives, then serve immediately.

INGREDIENTS

3-POUND CHICKEN

1½ QUARTS CHICKEN STOCK

4 LARGE TOMATOES, PEELED, SEEDED
    AND CHOPPED; OR 2 x 1-POUND
    CANS CHOPPED TOMATOES, DRAINED

2 MEDIUM-SIZED CORN COBS, CUT INTO
    3-INCH PIECES

2 MEDIUM YAMS, PEELED AND CHOPPED
    INTO 1-INCH THICK SLICES

2 SMALL POTATOES, PEELED AND CUT
    1-INCH THICK SLICES

4 OUNCES PEELED AND DICED PUMPKIN

⅔ CUP GREEN PEAS

2 SMALL FRESH CHILIES, SEEDED AND
    THINLY SLICED

2½ TEASPOONS SALT

FRESHLY GROUND BLACK PEPPER

1½ TABLESPOONS FINELY CHOPPED FRESH
    CHIVES

serves 6

Chilled salad soup ▶

Breadfruit Soup – CARIBBEAN

INGREDIENTS

¼ CUP BUTTER OR MARGARINE

1 MEDIUM ONION, FINELY CHOPPED

1 FAT GARLIC CLOVE, CRUSHED

1½ CUPS PEELED, CORED AND CHOPPED
  FRESH BREADFRUIT

2½ CUPS CHICKEN STOCK

1¼ CUPS LIGHT CREAM

1 TEASPOON SALT

¼ TEASPOON FRESHLY GROUND BLACK
  PEPPER

2 TEASPOONS FINELY CHOPPED FRESH
  PARSLEY, TO GARNISH

serves 6

METHOD

Melt the butter or margarine in a large saucepan. Add the onion and garlic, and cook for 5 minutes, stirring until they are soft. Add the breadfruit and chicken stock, and bring to a boil. Reduce the heat, and simmer for 20 minutes or until the breadfruit is tender. Put half the mixture in a blender or food processor, together with half of the cream, and blend them together. Tip the purée into a bowl. Repeat for the remainder of the mixture, using the remaining cream. Season the creamy purée with the salt and pepper. Chill the soup, and sprinkle with chopped parsley before serving.

Sidon Melon Soup – LEBANON

INGREDIENTS

2 LARGE OGEN MELONS, PEELED, SEEDED
  AND CHOPPED

4 TABLESPOONS LIME JUICE

4 TABLESPOONS FINE GRANULATED
  SUGAR

2 LARGE CANTALOUPE MELONS, PEELED,
  SEEDED AND CHOPPED

4 TABLESPOONS LEMON JUICE

½ CUP GREEK-STYLE YOGURT

GROUND CINNAMON, TO GARNISH

MINT LEAVES, TO GARNISH

serves 4

Melons of all types – green, yellow and orange – grow profusely on the small farms of the inland valleys and, until the Middle East crisis, were among the prime exports of the country. When at their peak, they are pleasing simply cut in half or quarters. This ingenious two-tone soup can make use of slightly over-ripe fruit.

METHOD

Purée the ogen melon, lime juice, and 2 tablespoons of sugar in a blender or food processor until smooth. Pour into a pitcher, cover and chill until cold. Rinse out the bowl of the blender, and fill with the cantaloupe melon, lemon juice and remaining sugar. Purée until smooth. Pour into a pitcher, cover and chill until cold. When ready to serve, position each soup bowl in front of you. Pick up both pitchers, and pour the two soups into the bowl at the same time, one on each side. Repeat with the remaining bowls. Each soup will be two-tone; use a spoon to feather the edges gently to obtain a softer effect. Top each serving with a dollop of yogurt sprinkled lightly with cinnamon and garnished with a sprig of mint.

Cucumber and Cumin Soup – MIDDLE EAST

Perfect for a hot day, this is a Levantine version of a soup popular throughout the Middle East, Turkey and the Balkans.

METHOD

Spread the cumin seeds on a baking sheet, and toast gently under the broiler until lightly colored. Turn the cumin seeds, chopped cucumbers, garlic, and buttermilk into a blender or food processor, and process until smooth. Pour the soup into a large bowl, season to taste, and chill for several hours. Serve the soup in bowls, with a thin slice of lemon floating on the

INGREDIENTS

½ TEASPOON CUMIN SEEDS

4 CUCUMBERS (ABOUT 1 POUND) PEELED, SEEDED AND CHOPPED

2 SMALL GARLIC CLOVES, CRUSHED

2 CUPS BUTTERMILK

SALT AND FRESHLY GROUND BLACK PEPPER

6 THIN SLICES LEMON, TO GARNISH

serves 6

Florida-style Mango Soup – AMERICA

The secret of this refreshing concoction is the seltzer and the extracts which enhance the flavors of the tropical fruits. Serve in small soup bowls set in larger bowls lined with crushed ice – or serve in frosted glass mugs.

METHOD

Purée the mango, star fruit, and pineapple in a blender or food processor until smooth. With motor running, add the soda, apricot nectar or juice, lime juice, and pineapple extract. Process until blended. Cover and chill until ready to serve. Float a star fruit slice in each serving, and garnish with mint leaves, if desired.

INGREDIENTS

1 SMALL MANGO, PEELED AND CUT INTO CHUNKS

3 STAR FRUIT, 2 CUT INTO SMALL PIECES AND 1 SLICED FOR GARNISH

⅛ MEDIUM PINEAPPLE, PEELED

½ CUP FIZZY LEMON-LIME SODA

⅓ CUP APRICOT NECTAR OR JUICE

2 TEASPOONS LIME JUICE

1 TEASPOON PINEAPPLE EXTRACT

FRESH MINT LEAVES, TO GARNISH (OPTIONAL)

serves 4 to 6

Dominican-style Tomato and Sweet Potato Soup – CARIBBEAN

INGREDIENTS

1 TABLESPOON OIL

1 TABLESPOON BUTTER OR MARGARINE

2 ONIONS, FINELY CHOPPED

1½ CUPS PEELED AND DICED SWEET
 POTATOES

1 POUND SKINNED AND FINELY
 CHOPPED TOMATOES

2½ CUPS CHICKEN STOCK

1 TEASPOON SALT

1 TEASPOON FRESH THYME, CHOPPED

JUICE AND GRATED RIND OF 1 ORANGE

JUICE AND GRATED RIND OF 1 LEMON
 OR LIME

FRESHLY GROUND BLACK PEPPER

SLICES OF LEMON, ORANGE AND
 TOMATO, TO GARNISH

serves 6

METHOD

Heat the oil and butter or margarine in a large saucepan. Add the onions, and cook them until they are soft. Add the sweet potatoes, tomatoes, chicken stock, salt, thyme, orange juice and rind, lemon or lime juice and rind, and freshly ground black pepper to taste. Bring to a boil, then lower the heat, cover the saucepan, and simmer for 25 minutes. Liquidize the soup in a blender or food processor, then return it to the saucepan, and simmer for 5 minutes longer to heat through. Serve it in warmed soup bowls, garnished with a slice of tomato, orange and lemon.

Dried Mushroom Soup – POLAND

Dried mushrooms are expensive, but they make a superb soup. In some households this special mushroom soup would be served as an alternative to beet soup on Christmas Eve; however, water could be used instead of beef stock.

INGREDIENTS

2 TABLESPOONS DRIED MUSHROOMS

2½ CUPS WATER

1 ONION, VERY FINELY CHOPPED

A LITTLE FAT OR BUTTER

3 TABLESPOONS ALL-PURPOSE FLOUR

1¼ CUPS BEEF STOCK

SALT AND FRESHLY GROUND
 BLACK PEPPER

1¼ CUPS SOUR CREAM

2 TABLESPOONS SNIPPED CHIVES

serves 4

METHOD

Place the mushrooms and water in a saucepan, and heat slowly until simmering. Cover and simmer for 5 minutes. Lift out the mushrooms with a slotted spoon. Press excess liquid from them, and chop finely. Strain the cooking liquor through cheesecloth, and reserve. Cook the onion in the minimum of fat in a saucepan over low heat for about 10 minutes, until soft but not browned. Stir in the flour, then slowly add the stock, stirring all the time. Pour in the reserved mushroom liquor, add the mushrooms, and stir well. Bring to a simmer, cover and cook for 30 minutes. Taste and season the soup, then stir in the sour cream, and heat slowly for a few minutes without boiling. Serve sprinkled with chives.

Icy Red Gazpacho – SPAIN

An icy, vinegared soup, made creamy with bread and oil, this soup probably dates back to the Romans. Bell peppers and tomatoes were added after Columbus' voyage. In Arab times it was prepared by pounding everything in a big stone mortar, but now every farm owns a battery whisk to chop the vegetables in a big, wide-mouthed bowl. In Spanish restaurants it is garnished with lots of extras from little bowls.

METHOD

Soak the bread in water, then squeeze out. Put it in a blender or food processor with the onion, garlic, olive oil, and salt, and purée. Add the cucumber to the blender or food processor with the bell pepper, then the tomatoes and vinegar (you may have to do this in two batches in a small machine). Chill for at least 12 hours, preferably overnight, or freeze for about 30 minutes. To serve, dilute with ice water (no ice cubes), and season to taste with the cayenne pepper. Arrange the garnishes in little dishes and pass them around on a tray for everyone to serve themselves.

INGREDIENTS

2 SLICES STALE WHITE BREAD, CRUSTS
   REMOVED
1 SMALL ONION, CHOPPED
2 GARLIC CLOVES, FINELY CHOPPED
2 TABLESPOONS OLIVE OIL
1 TEASPOON COARSE SALT
1 CUCUMBER, SEEDED AND CHOPPED,
   WITH SOME SKIN REMOVED
1 LARGE RED BELL PEPPER, SEEDED AND
   COARSELY CHOPPED
4–5 BIG RIPE RED TOMATOES, PEELED
   AND SEEDED
2 TABLESPOONS RED WINE OR SHERRY
   VINEGAR
3 CUPS ICE WATER
PINCH OF CAYENNE PEPPER

FOR THE GARNISHES

4 TABLESPOONS FRIED CROÛTONS
2 HARD-COOKED EGGS, PEELED AND
   CHOPPED
4 TABLESPOONS CHOPPED BELL PEPPER
   (RED, GREEN OR BOTH)
4 TABLESPOONS CHOPPED SPANISH
   ONION OR SCALLION
GREEN OR BLACK OLIVES, PITTED AND
   CHOPPED

serves 4

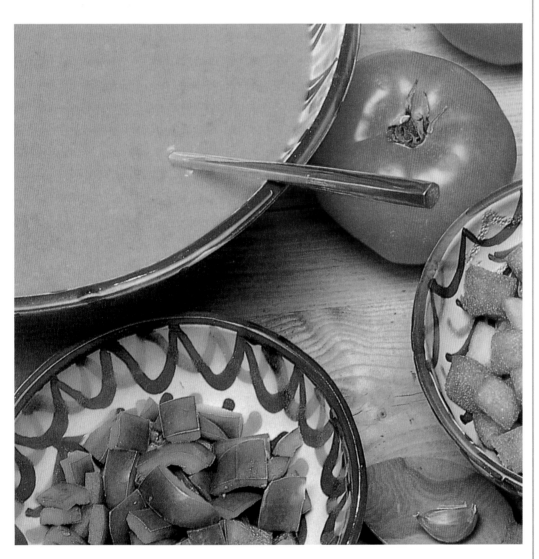

"Almost Nothing" Soup – UKRAINE

INGREDIENTS

3 POUNDS BEEF, CHICKEN, VEAL OR
  MIXED BONES

1 ONION, UNPEELED

SALT AND FRESHLY GROUND
  BLACK PEPPER

2 QUARTS WATER

2 POUNDS POTATOES, SCRUBBED AND
  DRIED

½ CUP BACON FAT OR MELTED BUTTER

½ CUP LIGHT CREAM (OPTIONAL)

2 TABLESPOONS CHOPPED FRESH CHIVES,
  TO GARNISH

serves 4 to 6

This soup, made from scraps, has a surprising flavor, smoky and nut-like. Add a little cream to make it more sophisticated.

METHOD

Place the bones, the unpeeled onion, and seasoning to taste in a large saucepan. Cover with the water, and put over high heat. Bring to a boil, then cover and simmer for 1 hour. Uncover and continue to simmer until the stock has reduced to almost half. Strain the stock, and return to the saucepan. Meanwhile, peel the potatoes. Reserve the potatoes themselves for another use. Melt the bacon fat or butter in a skillet and sauté the onion until soft, about 6 minutes. Add the potato skins, and continue to cook until they too are tender. Transfer the potato skins and onion to the saucepan containing the stock. Bring to a boil, then reduce the heat, and simmer for 10 minutes. Purée the soup in batches; return to the saucepan and reheat. Thin, if necessary, with a little water or the light cream. Ladle into individual bowls, and serve sprinkled with the chopped chives.

Lentil Soup – ITALY

METHOD

In a good sized pan, heat the olive oil over a medium heat. Very finely slice the onion, and soften it in the oil. Finely slice the celery, and add it to the onions when they are soft. Cook for 2 minutes or so. As the celery is cooking, dice the bacon. Add it to the mixture. Coarsely chop the tomatoes, and add them to the soup, together with the lentils. Crumble in the bouillon cube, and add 1½ quarts water. Bring to a boil on a high heat, and then reduce to a simmer. You must cook the soup until the lentils are tender, up to 45 minutes. Test by tasting the soup occasionally. When the lentils are soft, season with the salt. Off the heat, whisk in the butter and Parmesan. Pour the mixture into a suitable tureen, and generously coat the top with fresh black pepper.

INGREDIENTS

2 TABLESPOONS OLIVE OIL

1 MEDIUM ONION

1 CELERY STALK

2 SLICES BACON OR PANCETTA

1¼ CUPS BROWN OR GREEN LENTILS

1 BEEF BOUILLON CUBE

3 TABLESPOONS FRESHLY GRATED
 PARMESAN CHEESE

2 TABLESPOONS BUTTER

SALT AND FRESHLY GROUND
 BLACK PEPPER

serves 4 to 6

Hot and Sour Shrimp Soup – THAILAND

METHOD

Boil the stock in a pan, add the lemon grass and lime leaf, then the shrimp and mushrooms. When the shrimp are cooked, about 8 to 10 minutes, remove the pan from the heat and add the remaining ingredients. Let stand for 5 minutes, then check the seasoning, adding more fish sauce or lime juice, or breaking up the chilies to release more heat as required – the soup should be spicy-sour and a little salty. Serve accompanied by rice.

INGREDIENTS

3¾ CUPS CHICKEN STOCK

3 STALKS OF LEMON GRASS, CUT INTO
 ¼-INCH SLICES

3 KAFFIR LIME LEAVES

12 RAW MEDIUM-SIZED OR 6 LARGE
 SHRIMP, SHELLED BUT NOT DEHEADED

5 OUNCES MUSHROOMS, HALVED

5 FRESH SMALL WHOLE GREEN CHILIES

2 TABLESPOONS FRESH CHOPPED
 CILANTRO

3 TABLESPOONS LIME JUICE

½ TABLESPOON NUOC MAM SAUCE OR
 ½ TABLESPOON SOY SAUCE MIXED
 WITH A DASH OF ANCHOVY SAUCE

serves 4

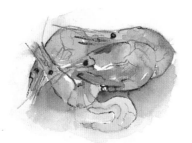

Bouillabaisse – FRANCE

Variations on this substantial soup – almost a fish stew – abound all over the Mediterranean, the only constant being to use as many different types of fish as you can lay your hands on.

INGREDIENTS

2½ POUNDS FISH

1 CUP SHELLFISH

4 TABLESPOONS OLIVE OIL

1 LARGE ONION, COARSELY CHOPPED

4 GARLIC CLOVES, CRUSHED

2 CUPS WINE

1 TABLESPOON FRESH MIXED HERBS

PINCH OF SAFFRON THREADS (OPTIONAL)

2 CUPS SKINNED, SEEDED AND COARSELY
    CHOPPED TOMATOES

1 TEASPOON SUGAR

SALT AND FRESHLY GROUND BLACK
    PEPPER

PINCH OF CAYENNE PEPPER

16 SLICES FRENCH BREAD FRIED IN OIL,
    TO SERVE

serves 8

METHOD

Clean the fish and cut into equal-sized hunks. Small fish can be left whole. Scrub any mussels or clams and debeard the mussels. Shell any shrimp and, if using scallops, cut the meat out of the shell and halve. Separate the fish onto two plates, one for firm-fleshed fish and one for soft-fleshed varieties. Keep any squid or inkfish separate. Heat the oil in a large saucepan, and fry the onion until it begins to brown. Add the garlic, and cook for several minutes. Add the wine, mixed herbs, and saffron. Simmer for 5 minutes, add any squid or inkfish, and cook for 10 minutes. Add the firm-fleshed fish, and cook for 10 minutes longer. Add the soft-fleshed fish, and simmer until almost cooked. You may need to add some water so that the liquid still covers the fish. Add the tomatoes, prepared shellfish,

and sugar, and season with salt, pepper and a little cayenne pepper. Cook for 5 minutes longer, by which time any clams or mussels will have opened. Serve with the fried bread and a good dollop of Aïoli in each bowl.

Smoked Fish Soup – THAILAND

INGREDIENTS

4 CUPS CHICKEN STOCK

2 TABLESPOONS SLICED GALANGAL

2 STALKS OF LEMON GRASS, CUT INTO
    1½-INCH PIECES AND CRUSHED
    LIGHTLY

1 TEASPOON SHRIMP PASTE

9 OUNCES DRIED SMOKED FISH
    (NOT SALTED), BONES REMOVED AND
    BROKEN INTO 3 OR 4 PIECES

2 TABLESPOONS SLIGHTLY CRUSHED
    SHALLOT

1½ TEASPOONS TAMARIND OR LIME JUICE

¼ CUP SWEET BASIL LEAVES

1 TABLESPOON NUOC MAM SAUCE OR
    1 TABLESPOON SOY SAUCE MIXED
    WITH ½ TABLESPOON ANCHOVY
    SAUCE

½ TEASPOON SALT

5 DRIED RED CHILIES, DRY-FRIED FOR
    3–5 MINUTES

serves 4 to 6

METHOD

Pour the chicken stock into a pan, bring to a boil, and add the galangal, lemon grass, and shrimp paste. Boil again for 2 minutes, and then add the dried fish pieces, shallot, and tamarind juice. Bring back to a boil, and simmer for 5 minutes; then remove from the heat, and add the remaining ingredients. Mix and season to taste with more tamarind, lime juice, or fish sauce, if you like. Leave for 10 minutes before serving.

Ham and Corn Chowder – AMERICA

INGREDIENTS

2 PORK KNUCKLES (ABOUT 1½ POUNDS)

1 MEDIUM ONION, QUARTERED

2 CELERY STALKS, CUT INTO
   3-INCH PIECES

2 CARROTS, CUT INTO 3-INCH PIECES

SEVERAL SPRIGS OF FRESH PARSLEY

1 BAY LEAF

3 CUPS CHICKEN STOCK

3 CUPS CORN KERNELS

½ TEASPOON CUMIN

⅛ TEASPOON CAYENNE PEPPER

⅛ TEASPOON WHITE PEPPER

1 CUP HEAVY CREAM

⅓ CUP CHOPPED SCALLIONS

2 TABLESPOONS CHOPPED RED BELL
   PEPPER

serves 4 to 6

Ham and corn are such integral parts of Southern cuisine that we combined them in this inexpensive corn chowder. Use fresh corn if it is available, or frozen if not. The last-minute addition of scallions and red bell peppers adds crunch and color.

METHOD

Place the knuckles, onion, celery, carrots, parsley, and bay leaf in a large pan, and cover with water. Bring to a boil, and simmer for about 1½ hours. Remove the knuckle, and cut off the meat. Return the bones to the pan, and continue reducing the broth. Cut the knuckle meat into strips. Strain the pork broth, and discard the vegetables. Combine 1 cup of the pork broth in a large saucepan with the chicken stock. Bring to a boil. Add the corn, pork, and spices, and simmer for 20 minutes. Add the cream, scallions, and red bell peppers, and bring just barely to the boiling point. Taste and adjust for seasoning. The pork is salty, and should provide enough salt.

Louisiana-style Black Bean Soup – AMERICA

INGREDIENTS

2½ CUPS DRIED BLACK BEANS

2 TABLESPOONS VEGETABLE OIL

2 CUPS CHOPPED ONIONS

6 GARLIC CLOVES, FINELY CHOPPED

¾ CUP DICED CELERY

2 QUARTS CHICKEN STOCK

HAM BONE OR 1–2 PORK KNUCKLES

2 TEASPOONS GROUND CUMIN

¼ TEASPOON CAYENNE PEPPER

2 TEASPOONS DRIED OREGANO

2 TEASPOONS BROWN SUGAR

1 TABLESPOON LIME JUICE

½ RED BELL PEPPER, CHOPPED

2 TABLESPOONS SHERRY

1 POUND ANDOUILLE SAUSAGE, SLICED

SOUR CREAM

CHOPPED SCALLIONS

CHOPPED FRESH CILANTRO

serves 8

This is a hearty, spicy soup. This recipe calls for Andouille sausage, a very spicy smoked Louisiana sausage. You can substitute another sausage, but be sure to leave time to cook it if it's uncooked. The soup is good without the sausage, too.

METHOD

Pick through the dry beans for pebbles. Put the beans in a large pan, adding water several inches deeper than the beans. Put the pan on the stove and bring the water to a boil. Remove from the heat, and let the beans sit for 1 hour. Pour off the water, and rinse well. In a skillet, sauté the onion, garlic, and celery in oil until the vegetables are tender, about 5 minutes. Return the beans to the pan. Add the chicken stock, sautéed vegetables, and ham bone or pork knuckles. Bring the beans to a boil, reduce the heat and let the beans simmer, uncovered, for 1 hour. Add the cumin, cayenne pepper, oregano, brown sugar, lime juice, red bell pepper, and sherry. Simmer the beans over low heat until they are tender, about 30 minutes longer. Add water or chicken stock if necessary, as the beans must not dry out, and there should be some

excess liquid. Purée the soup in batches in a blender or food processor. Return the purée to the pan, and reheat. Add the sausage, and simmer for about 10 minutes longer. To serve, top each bowl with a dollop of sour cream, and garnish with cilantro, and scallions.

Chlodnik – POLAND

INGREDIENTS

1 SMALL ONION, FINELY CHOPPED

1 GARLIC CLOVE, CRUSHED (OPTIONAL)

A LITTLE FAT OR BUTTER

4 CUPS SHREDDED YOUNG BEET LEAVES,
    SWISS CHARD OR SPINACH

1¼ CUPS CHICKEN STOCK

1 CUCUMBER, PEELED AND THINLY
    SLICED (ABOUT 1 POUND)

2 TEASPOONS SUGAR

1 TABLESPOON LEMON JUICE

SALT AND FRESHLY GROUND BLACK
    PEPPER

1¼ CUPS NATURAL YOGURT

1¼ CUPS SOUR CREAM

4 EGGS, HARD-COOKED, CHOPPED

4 SMALL BEETS, COOKED, PEELED AND
    COARSELY CHOPPED

2 TABLESPOONS CHOPPED FRESH DILL

2 TABLESPOONS SNIPPED CHIVES

serves 4 to 6

Chlodnik is a summery soup, made when the beets are very young and their leaves are tender. In Poland, sour milk – made by adding a culture as when making sour cream – is used instead of the combination of yogurt and sour cream included here.

METHOD

Cook the onion and garlic in the minimum of fat in a large saucepan for about 10 to 15 minutes over low heat, until very soft but not browned. Stir in the shredded leaves, and pour in the stock. Bring to a boil, reduce the heat, and cover the pan. Simmer for 15 minutes, or until the leaves are tender. Let cool, then chill. Stir in the cucumber, sugar, lemon juice, and seasoning. Add the yogurt and sour cream, stir well and taste for seasoning. Extra lemon juice may be added if liked. Ladle the soup into bowls, add the eggs, beets and herbs, then serve at once.

Lemon Chicken Soup – LEBANON

INGREDIENTS

3–4 POUND FREE-RANGE CHICKEN, CUT
    INTO PIECES

2½ CUPS CHICKEN STOCK

1 MEDIUM ONION, CHOPPED

2 LARGE BEEF TOMATOES, PEELED,
    SEEDED AND CHOPPED

1 TABLESPOON FRESH TARRAGON

1 TEASPOON GRATED LEMON RIND

SALT AND FRESHLY GROUND
    BLACK PEPPER

2 CYPRUS POTATOES, PEELED AND
    CHOPPED

8 OUNCES OKRA, TRIMMED

½ CUP CHOPPED CANNED JALAPEÑO
    CHILIES

⅓ CUP FROZEN CORN KERNELS

JUICE OF 1 LEMON

FLAT-LEAFED PARSLEY, TO GARNISH

PINCH OF PAPRIKA, TO GARNISH

serves 4

Chickens in the peasant areas of Lebanon are very much free range and, since they are valued for their eggs, can live to a ripe age (for a chicken!). Older hens find their way into soups like this one.

METHOD

In a large casserole, combine the chicken pieces (except for the breasts), the stock, onion, tomatoes, tarragon, and rind. Pour over 3 cups of water, season to taste, and bring to a boil. Reduce the heat, cover and simmer for 20 minutes. Add the breasts, and continue to cook until the breasts are just cooked through. Remove all the chicken pieces from the soup with a slotted spoon, and set them aside to cool. Add the potatoes to the soup, cover and continue to simmer until the potatoes are done, about 25 minutes; add the okra after 10 minutes. When the chicken is cool enough to handle, remove the meat from the bones, discarding the skin. Chop the meat into small pieces. Add to the soup, together with the chilies and corn. Bring the soup back to a boil, reduce the heat, and simmer for 5 minutes longer. Stir in the lemon juice and serve immediately, garnished with chopped parsley and paprika to taste.

Sauerkraut Soup – POLAND

INGREDIENTS

8 OUNCES PORK BELLY, RIND REMOVED

1 LARGE ONION, CHOPPED

1 LEEK, THINLY SLICED

1 CARROT, DICED

4 CUPS STOCK, SUCH AS BEEF, CHICKEN
    OR VEAL

1½ CUPS SAUERKRAUT

1 POTATO, DICED

SALT AND FRESHLY GROUND BLACK
    PEPPER

serves 4 to 6

Kapusniak by name, here is another of Poland's popular soups. For authenticity, add all the juices from the sauerkraut to give the soup a sour flavor. However, if you are unused to the tang of authentic Polish dishes, squeeze out the sauerkraut as in this recipe.

METHOD

Dice the pork, then cook it over a low heat in a large, heavy-bottomed saucepan until the fat runs. Add the onion and leek. Continue to cook, stirring frequently, until the onion is slightly softened but not browned. Stir in the carrot, and pour in the stock; then bring to a boil. Reduce the heat, cover and simmer for 30 minutes. Drain the sauerkraut, reserving the juice, and squeeze out all the remaining juice. Use a sharp knife to slice across the pat of squeezed sauerkraut. Add the sauerkraut to the soup with the potato and some seasoning. Stir well and simmer, covered, for 30 minutes longer. Taste and adjust the seasoning. Stir in some or all of the juice reserved from the sauerkraut, according to taste. Serve piping hot.

Sorrel Soup with Kidneys and Gherkins – RUSSIAN FEDERATION

INGREDIENTS

⅓ CUP BUTTER

¼ CUP VEGETABLE OR SUNFLOWER OIL

1 MEDIUM ONION, FINELY CHOPPED

1 CELERY STALK, FINELY CHOPPED

1 MEDIUM CARROT, FINELY CHOPPED

1 LARGE POTATO, PEELED AND DICED

1 POUND LAMB KIDNEYS, TRIMMED AND
    CUT INTO ½-INCH PIECES

½ CUP ALL-PURPOSE FLOUR

6 PARSLEY SPRIGS, CHOPPED

2 POUNDS FRESH SORREL LEAVES OR 1
    POUND EACH SORREL AND YOUNG
    SPINACH LEAVES, STRIPPED FROM
    THEIR STEMS AND FINELY CHOPPED

SALT AND FRESHLY GROUND
    BLACK PEPPER

1½ QUARTS BEEF STOCK

1 BAY LEAF

2 SOUR GHERKINS, FINELY CHOPPED
    WITH ⅓ CUP PICKLING JUICES

1 EGG YOLK

SOUR CREAM

serves 8

METHOD

Melt ¼ cup butter and 2 tablespoons oil in a large saucepan, and gently sauté the onion, celery, and carrot until they are softened and lightly colored, about 10 minutes. Add the diced potato, and continue cooking, stirring for 5 minutes longer. Transfer the vegetables to a bowl, and set aside. Heat the remaining butter and oil in the pan. Dip the kidney pieces into the flour, and slowly fry them until they are slightly browned, about 3 minutes. Remove with a slotted spoon, and set aside. Stir the parsley and sorrel (or sorrel and spinach) into the pan, and add the cooked vegetables. Toss everything gently until the leaves are wilted. Season to taste with salt and pepper, and add the beef stock and bay leaf. Bring to a boil; then cover, lower the heat, and simmer for about 25 minutes. Remove the bay leaf, and mash the vegetables to thicken the soup. Stir in the gherkins and their juice, together with the cooked kidneys. Simmer for 5 minutes longer. Remove a cupful of the soup, and beat with the egg yolk in a small bowl. Stir the egg mixture back into the soup, and heat it briefly. Do not boil, or the egg will curdle. If serving hot, transfer the soup to a large tureen, and pass the sour cream separately. If serving cold, cool to room temperature, then chill for 2 to 3 hours before dividing between individual bowls, each topped with a spoonful of sour cream.

Won Ton Soup — CHINA

INGREDIENTS

1½ CUPS GROUND PORK

4 SCALLIONS, FINELY CHOPPED

2 BUTTON MUSHROOMS, FINELY
  CHOPPED

2 TABLESPOONS SOY SAUCE

1 TEASPOON SESAME OIL

½ QUANTITY WON TON DOUGH (SEE
  PAGE 112)

CORNSTARCH, FOR DUSTING

1 EGG, BEATEN

1 TABLESPOON OIL

1 BONELESS CHICKEN BREAST, SKINNED
  AND DICED

2 LEEKS, SLICED

3¼ CUPS GOOD CHICKEN STOCK

4 TABLESPOONS DRY SHERRY

SALT AND FRESHLY GROUND
  BLACK PEPPER

serves 4

METHOD

Mix the pork, scallions, mushrooms, soy sauce, and sesame oil. Roll out the dough into a 15-inch square, dusting the surface with cornstarch as necessary. The dough should be very thin. Cut the dough into 3-inch strips, then across into squares. Cover the dough with plastic wrap. To fill the won tons, roll a square of dough again so that it is paper-thin. Shape a little meat into a ball, and place it in the middle of the dough square. Brush the meat with egg, then fold the dough around it, and pinch it together to seal in the meat. Leave the corners of the dough hanging free. Fill all the won tons in the same way, and place them on a platter or board dusted with cornstarch. For the soup, heat the oil in a saucepan. Add the chicken and leeks, and cook, stirring often, for 20 minutes, until the leek is softened and the chicken is just cooked. Pour in the stock, and bring to a boil. Cover and simmer for 20 minutes. Stir in the sherry, and seasoning to taste. Add the won tons to the soup, bring back to a boil, and reduce the heat slightly so that it does not boil fiercely. Cook for 5 minutes. Test a won ton to make sure the filling is cooked, then ladle the soup and won tons into bowls.

7

Salads

~

Nuevo Cubano Fruited Crab Salad – AMERICA

INGREDIENTS

1 LARGE FRESH PINEAPPLE, OR
   1-POUND CAN UNSWEETENED
   PINEAPPLE, CUT INTO BITE-SIZED
   CHUNKS, DRAINED

2 POUNDS CRAB MEAT, CUT INTO
   CHUNKS, OR OCEAN STICKS
   OR CRAB STICKS

1 LARGE MANGO, PEELED AND CUBED

1½ CUPS ORANGE-FLESH MELON BALLS

2 CUPS SEEDLESS GRAPES

YOGURT OR SOUR CREAM TO SERVE
   (OPTIONAL)

serves 4

Ocean sticks or crab sticks work well in this salad because when served cold in a non-cook dish, the white-fish based dish is very similar to more expensive crab meat. Of course, if you prefer to use real crab meat, by all means do so. If using fresh pineapple, cut lengthwise into quarters, cutting through crown, remove fruit from shells, discard core and reserve shells to use as "pineapple boats."

METHOD

Combine pineapple, crab meat or ocean sticks, mango, orange-flesh melon balls, and grapes. Place in your pineapple boats or in a glass bowl.

Chill until ready to serve. Serve with yogurt or sour cream, if liked.

Simple Salad – VIETNAM

INGREDIENTS

1 LETTUCE, FINELY SHREDDED

1 CUCUMBER, PEELED AND CUT
   LENGTHWAYS INTO THIN STRIPS

2 CARROTS, PEELED AND CUT
   LENGTHWAYS INTO THIN STRIPS

1 LARGE HANDFUL OF BEAN SPROUTS,
   WASHED AND DRAINED THOROUGHLY

3 TABLESPOONS CHOPPED FRESH
   CILANTRO

3 TABLESPOONS CHOPPED FRESH MINT

2 HARD-COOKED EGGS

2 HARD-COOKED EGGS, QUARTERED, TO
   GARNISH

FOR THE SALAD DRESSING

4 TABLESPOONS NUOC MAM SAUCE OR
   3 TABLESPOONS LIGHT SOY SAUCE
   MIXED WITH 1 TEASPOON ANCHOVY
   SAUCE

4 TABLESPOONS LEMON JUICE

1 TABLESPOON WINE VINEGAR

3 GARLIC CLOVES, FINELY CHOPPED AND
   CRUSHED

1 TEASPOON SUGAR

1 FRESH RED CHILI, FINELY CHOPPED

3 TABLESPOONS CRUSHED ROASTED
   PEANUTS

serves 4

METHOD

Combine the lettuce, cucumber, carrots, and bean sprouts. Mix lightly. Mix the Nuoc Mam sauce, lemon juice, and vinegar. Add the garlic and sugar, and stir thoroughly, then add the chili

and peanuts, and stir again. Toss the dressing into the salad, and scatter the cilantro and mint over the top. Garnish with the egg quarters.

Tomato Salad with Mediterranean Vinaigrette – SPAIN

INGREDIENTS

3 BEEF TOMATOES

½ ONION, FINELY SLICED

A FEW BLACK OLIVES

FOR THE DRESSING

½ CUP BRINE FROM A JAR OF OLIVES OR
    GHERKINS

¾ CUP RED WINE VINEGAR

⅔ CUP OLIVE OIL

1 TEASPOON GARLIC

1 TEASPOON SUGAR

1 TEASPOON SALT

1 TEASPOON BLACK PEPPER

serves 4

This is lovely in summer with cheese and cold beer, or with anchovy fillets layered between the tomato and onion.

METHOD

Slice the tomatoes horizontally. Arrange either in a large bowl with onion in between layers, or on a large plate. Sprinkle with black olives. Mix all the dressing ingredients together, and let marinate for at least 30 minutes. Dredge the tomatoes with the dressing and serve. If keeping to serve later, add the dressing just 20 minutes before required.

Salad with Roquefort Dressing – SPAIN

The magic attraction of Roquefort cheese for the Basques is that it touches the same taste nerve as salt cod! Roquefort dressings are fashionable in Madrid too, and this one is first class.

METHOD

Arrange the lettuce in a wide, shallow salad bowl. Whisk the first three dressing ingredients together; then work in the oil, and season to taste with pepper and paprika or cayenne pepper. Pour over the salad, and garnish the top with egg and ham.

INGREDIENTS

1–2 LETTUCE, PREFERABLY ROMAINE, WASHED, CUT ACROSS IN HAND WIDTHS AND CHILLED

1 HARD-COOKED EGG, PEELED AND CHOPPED

2 TABLESPOONS SHREDDED RAW SERRANO HAM (OR SUBSTITUTE 4 TABLESPOONS DICED FRIED HAM)

FOR THE ROQUEFORT DRESSING

2 TABLESPOONS CRUMBLED ROQUEFORT CHEESE

2 TABLESPOONS HEAVY CREAM

2 TABLESPOONS WHITE WINE VINEGAR

6–8 TABLESPOONS VIRGIN OLIVE OIL

FRESHLY GROUND BLACK PEPPER

PINCH OF HOT PAPRIKA OR CAYENNE PEPPER

serves 4 to 6

Coleslaw – ENGLAND

Use a combination of red and white cabbage for color. Prepare this several hours ahead to give the flavors time to blend.

METHOD

Combine the vegetables in a salad bowl, and toss well. Whisk together the remaining ingredients in a small bowl; then taste and adjust the seasonings. Mix with the slaw, cover and refrigerate until ready to serve.

INGREDIENTS

3 CUPS SHREDDED CABBAGE

3 CARROTS, PEELED AND GRATED

3 SCALLIONS, FINELY CHOPPED

½ LARGE GREEN BELL PEPPER, CUT INTO THIN STRIPS

½ CUP MAYONNAISE

½ CUP SOUR CREAM

¼ CUP WHITE WINE VINEGAR

1 TABLESPOON SUGAR

1 TABLESPOON CHOPPED FRESH PARSLEY

1 TEASPOON CELERY SEED

1 TABLESPOON GRATED ONION

PINCH OF SALT

PINCH OF FRESHLY GROUND BLACK PEPPER

serves 4

Hot Chicken Liver Salad – CHINA

INGREDIENTS

8 OUNCES CHICKEN LIVERS

½ TEASPOON GROUND CORIANDER

¼ TEASPOON GROUND MACE

¼ TEASPOON PAPRIKA

1 TABLESPOON ALL-PURPOSE FLOUR

SALT AND FRESHLY GROUND
  BLACK PEPPER

2 SCALLIONS, CHOPPED

4 TABLESPOONS CHOPPED FRESH
  PARSLEY

1 TEASPOON GRATED LEMON RIND

10 DICED RINDLESS BACON SLICES

2 TABLESPOONS OLIVE OIL

SALAD OF MIXED LEAVES, TO SERVE

LEMON WEDGES, TO GARNISH

serves 4

This is equally good as a light lunch or for supper.

METHOD

Rinse, drain and dry the chicken livers on paper towels. Trim any membranes from them, then halve or quarter each piece of liver. Sprinkle the coriander, mace, paprika, flour, and plenty of seasoning over the livers, and mix well to coat all the pieces. Mix the scallions with the parsley and lemon rind, then set aside. Prepare the salad bases for serving the chicken livers. Place the diced bacon in a cold pan, and stir-fry over medium to high heat until the fat from the bacon runs. Continue to stir-fry until all the bacon dice have become browned and are crisp. Use a slotted spoon to remove them from the pan, and then drain the dice on paper towels. Add the olive oil to the fat remaining in the pan, and heat it briefly; then add the chicken livers with all

their seasonings. Stir-fry until firm, lightly browned and cooked – which should take about 5 minutes. Mix in the crispy bacon and the scallion mixture. Spoon the chicken livers onto the prepared salads. Garnish the dish with lemon wedges for their juice, and serve it at once, with Melba toast.

To make Melba toast

Lightly toast medium-thick bread slices on both sides. Cut off the crusts, and slice each piece through horizontally to give two very thin slices. Toast the uncooked sides of the bread well away from the heat source until lightly browned and slightly curled. Cool on a wire rack.

Israeli Salad – ISRAEL

This simple salad of diced fresh vegetables and olive oil is eaten everywhere in Israel, as an accompaniment to broiled chicken and meats, in pocket bread, and is even eaten for breakfast in some homes. You can add any vegetables you like, but tomato and cucumber are essentials. The vegetables should be cut into very small dice, about ¼-inch pieces.

INGREDIENTS

2 LARGE RIPE TOMATOES, CUT INTO
   ¼-IN CUBES
1 LARGE, OR 2 SMALL, CUCUMBERS,
   PEELED AND DICED
1 GREEN BELL PEPPER, CORED, SEEDED
   AND DICED
1 ONION, CHOPPED
4 TABLESPOONS CHOPPED FRESH
   PARSLEY
2–3 TABLESPOONS OLIVE OIL
JUICE OF 1 LEMON
PINCH OF SALT
FRESHLY GROUND BLACK PEPPER
FRESH MINT LEAVES, TO GARNISH

serves 4

METHOD

Combine cubed tomato, diced cucumber, green bell pepper, onion, and parsley, in a large salad bowl and toss together. Sprinkle with olive oil, lemon juice, and salt and pepper to taste, and toss again. Garnish with fresh mint.

Variation

Prepare vegetables as above but dress with 3 to 4 tablespoons of Tahini, diluted with 2 tablespoons lemon juice and seasoned with salt and pepper. Thin to the desired consistency with a little water or more lemon juice.

Cucumber Salad – AMERICA

Use bought cucumbers or ones from your garden, either will work well. This salad benefits from a couple hours of marinating.

METHOD

Put the cucumbers, onions and bell pepper in a bowl. Make the dressing by combining the remaining ingredients, then whisk or shake well. Pour the dressing over the salad.

INGREDIENTS

2 LARGE CUCUMBERS, PEELED AND
   THINLY SLICED
½ SWEET ONION, THINLY SLICED
½ RED BELL PEPPER, CUT INTO JULIENNE
   STRIPS
⅓ CUP OLIVE OIL
2 TABLESPOONS LEMON JUICE
1 GARLIC CLOVE, CRUSHED
2 TEASPOONS FINELY CHOPPED FRESH
   PARSLEY
1 FINELY CHOPPED FRESH TARRAGON
¼ TEASPOON SALT AND FRESHLY
   GROUND BLACK PEPPER

serves 4

Herring and Apple Salad – POLAND

Salted herrings and rollmops are widely used in southern Poland where fresh fish rarely makes an appearance in shops or on menus. This salad may be served as an appetizer or as a light main dish.

INGREDIENTS

3 SALTED HERRING FILLETS

¼ CUCUMBER, PEELED AND THINLY
   SLICED (ABOUT 4 OUNCES)

½ ONION, THINLY SLICED

1 PICKLED CUCUMBER, THINLY SLICED

2 CRISP, GREEN EATING APPLES, CORED,
   QUARTERED AND THINLY SLICED

1 TEASPOON CIDER VINEGAR

1 TABLESPOON CHOPPED FRESH DILL

4 TABLESPOONS SOUR CREAM

serves 4

METHOD

Remove any bones from the herring fillets, then cut them into small strips. Mix the herring, cucumber, onion, pickled cucumber, and apple with the vinegar. Spoon the mixture onto a plate, and sprinkle with dill. Trickle the sour cream over the salad, and serve at once.

Classic Feta Salad – GREECE

The secret of this internationally famous salad is not in its method, but in the ingredients. You need the freshest of everything to create the feeling of lazy days in the Mediterranean sunshine.

INGREDIENTS

2 LARGE, RIPE TOMATOES

½ CUCUMBER, DICED

1 GREEN BELL PEPPER, SEEDED AND
   SLICED INTO RINGS

⅓ CUP KALAMATA OLIVES

1 LARGE RED ONION, FINELY SLICED

6 OUNCES FETA CHEESE, CUT INTO
   ½-INCH CUBES

FINELY GRATED RIND AND JUICE OF
   ½ LEMON

¼ CUP OLIVE OIL

1 TEASPOON DRIED OREGANO

PINCH OF COARSELY GROUND SALT

serves 4 to 6

METHOD

Cut the tomatoes into thin wedges, and place in a medium-sized bowl. Add the cucumber, green bell pepper, and olives. Toss the salad together with half of the red onion slices and half of the cubed feta. Scatter the remaining onions and feta over the top of the salad. Sprinkle over the lemon rind and juice, douse with the olive oil, and season with the oregano and salt. Gently toss the salad once just before serving.

Spicy Seafood Salad — THAILAND

The Thai versions of salad, of which this is one, are flavorful assemblies of different ingredients quite unlike those we are accustomed to in the West. Most are extremely spicy. This "yam" combines three of the basic five flavors: spicy, sour and salty.

INGREDIENTS

5 OUNCES SEA BASS OR PERCH, CLEANED, GUTTED AND SLICED THINLY INTO STRIPS

⅔ CUP SHELLED SHRIMP

5 OUNCES SQUID, BODY AND TENTACLES, CLEANED, GUTTED AND SLICED INTO ¾-INCH STRIPS

7 SMALL FRESH GREEN CHILIES

5 GARLIC CLOVES

2 CILANTRO ROOTS

2 TABLESPOONS NUOC MAM SAUCE OR 2 TABLESPOONS LIGHT SOY SAUCE MIXED WITH ½ TABLESPOON ANCHOVY SAUCE

½ TEASPOON SUGAR

2 TABLESPOONS LIME OR LEMON JUICE

4 SCALLIONS, SLICED INTO ¼-INCH PIECES

1 CUP THINLY SLICED ONIONS

½ CUP SLICED CELERY LEAVES AND STALKS

serves **6**

METHOD

Cook the fish, shrimp and squid separately in salted water until cooked, about 2 to 3 minutes each, and drain. Pound the chilies, garlic, cilantro root, fish sauce, and sugar together with a pestle and mortar until fine. Place in a bowl and mix in the lemon juice, scallions, onion and celery. Stir in the fish and seafood, and mix well. Serve immediately.

Trinidad Salt Cod Salad – CARIBBEAN

INGREDIENTS

8 OUNCES SALT COD, SOAKED
    OVERNIGHT AND DRAINED

JUICE OF 1 LIME OR LEMON

1 ONION, FINELY CHOPPED

3 TOMATOES, CHOPPED

3 TABLESPOONS OLIVE OIL

2 HARD-COOKED EGGS, CHOPPED

1 FRESH CHILI, SEEDED AND FINELY
    CHOPPED

2 TABLESPOONS FINELY CHOPPED
    SCALLIONS

1 GREEN BELL PEPPER, SEEDED AND
    FINELY CHOPPED

2 TABLESPOONS FINELY CHOPPED FRESH
    PARSLEY

FRESHLY GROUND BLACK PEPPER

serves 6

METHOD

Boil the cod for 20 minutes, or until it flakes. Drain off the water, and rinse under cold running water. Remove the skin and bones, and flake the fish. Put the flaked fish into a glass bowl. Add the lime or lemon juice, onion, tomatoes, olive oil, eggs, chili, scallions, green bell pepper, parsley, and freshly ground black pepper, and mix well. When the mixture has cooled, cover the bowl with plastic wrap, and refrigerate overnight. Serve the next day on crackers, fresh bread or small, toasted slices of bread.

Florida-style Lobster-Mango Chutney – AMERICA

The subtle sweetness of lobster and mango pair beautifully with hints of spiciness and tartness in the vinaigrette dressing in this dish.

METHOD

To make the vinaigrette, combine the juice and rind of the lime. Whisk in the curry powder, safflower oil, and seasoning. Stir well. Just before serving, toss the lobster, celery, 1½ cups mango chunks and the vinaigrette together. Mound remaining mango chunks in the center of lettuce-lined plates, and top with the lobster-mango mixture. Garnish, if liked, and serve.

INGREDIENTS

1 x 10 OUNCE CAN LOBSTER, DRAINED, TORN INTO ½-INCH PIECES AND THEN CHILLED

1½ CUPS THINLY SLICED CELERY

4 CUPS CHOPPED FRESH MANGO, OR DRAINED CANNED MANGO, CHILLED

4 ROMAINE, RED OAK LEAF, LOLLO ROSSO OR BOSTON LETTUCE LEAVES

4 TEASPOONS THINLY SLICED SCALLIONS

FOR THE CURRY-LIME VINAIGRETTE

1½ TABLESPOONS FINELY GRATED LIME RIND

3–4 TABLESPOONS LIME JUICE

4 TABLESPOONS CURRY POWDER

½ CUP SAFFLOWER OIL

SALT AND FRESHLY GROUND WHITE PEPPER

PAPAYA SEEDS (OPTIONAL), TO GARNISH

serves 4

Eastern Pasta Salad – POLAND

INGREDIENTS

12 OUNCES DRIED PASTA

DASH OF OLIVE OIL

14-OUNCE CAN GARABANZO BEANS,
    DRAINED

4 TABLESPOONS CHOPPED FRESH MINT

FINELY GRATED RIND OF 1 LEMON

FOR THE DRESSING

3 GARLIC CLOVES, CRUSHED

6 TABLESPOONS EXTRA VIRGIN OLIVE OIL

3 TABLESPOONS WHITE WINE VINEGAR

JUICE OF 1 LEMON

SALT AND FRESHLY GROUND
    BLACK PEPPER

serves 4 to 6

A traditional combination of mint and lemon makes this dish a salad for summer. Choose your favorite pasta shapes for this recipe, and serve with warm pocket bread to mop up the delicious dressing.

METHOD

Bring a large saucepan of water to a boil, and add the pasta with a dash of olive oil. Cook for about 10 minutes, stirring occasionally, until tender. Drain and rinse under cold running water. Drain again and place in a large mixing bowl. Add the garabanzo beans, mint and lemon rind to the pasta. Place all the dressing ingredients in a screw-top jar, and shake well to mix. Pour the dressing over the bean mixture, and mix well to combine. Cover and chill for at least 30 minutes. Toss before serving.

Florida-style Curried Tuna Salad with Tropical Fruit – AMERICA

METHOD

Combine the tuna, mango or papaya, celery, papaya seeds, if using, half the carrots, and spring and red onion in a bowl. Combine the mayonnaise and curry powder in a small bowl; then add to the tuna mixture, and toss gently to mix. Cover and chill. Spoon the salad into a lettuce-lined serving dish. Sprinkle the remaining carrot over the salad for garnish.

INGREDIENTS

2 x 6½-OUNCE CANS TUNA IN BRINE, DRAINED AND FLAKED

1¼ CUPS DICED AND WELL-DRAINED MANGO OR PAPAYA

1½ CUPS CHOPPED CELERY

⅓ CUP PAPAYA SEEDS, GROUND TO SIZE OF PEPPERCORNS (OPTIONAL)

1 CUP GRATED CARROTS

2 TABLESPOONS CHOPPED SCALLIONS

2 TABLESPOONS CHOPPED RED ONION

¾ CUP MAYONNAISE

½ TEASPOON CURRY POWDER

LETTUCE LEAVES

serves 4 to 6

Spicy Mussel Salad – THAILAND

METHOD

Mix together all the ingredients except the cabbage in a bowl. Taste for seasoning, adding extra lime juice or fish sauce if you like. Serve on a platter, with the cabbage leaves around the edge to be eaten with the salad.

INGREDIENTS

2 CUPS COOKED MUSSEL MEAT (STEAM APPROX. 2 QUARTS MUSSELS IN THEIR SHELLS AND REMOVE MEAT)

10 SMALL FRESH GREEN CHILIES, FINELY CHOPPED

2 TABLESPOONS MINT LEAVES

3 TABLESPOONS LIME OR LEMON JUICE

2½ TABLESPOONS NUOC MAM SAUCE OR 2 TABLESPOONS LIGHT SOY SAUCE MIXED WITH ½ TABLESPOON ANCHOVY SAUCE

2 TABLESPOONS SLICED SHALLOTS

2 TABLESPOONS GINGER ROOT CUT INTO MATCHSTICKS

2 TABLESPOONS FINELY SHREDDED LEMON GRASS

½ TABLESPOON SHREDDED KAFFIR LIME LEAF

1 SMALL HEAD OF WHITE CHINESE CABBAGE, CUT INTO WEDGES

½ SMALL HEAD OF GREEN CABBAGE, CUT INTO WEDGES

serves 4

Ground Meat, Crab and Grapefruit Salad – VIETNAM

INGREDIENTS

GENEROUS 1 CUP GROUND PORK OR
    BEEF

3 TABLESPOONS WATER

2 TABLESPOONS LIME OR LEMON JUICE

2 TABLESPOONS NUOC MAM SAUCE OR

2 TABLESPOONS MAGGI LIQUID
    SEASONING MIXED WITH 1 TEASPOON
    ANCHOVY SAUCE

1 FRESH GREEN CHILI, FINELY SLICED

1 SMALL SPANISH ONION, FINELY DICED

½-INCH PIECE FRESH GINGER ROOT,
    FINELY CHOPPED

1 TABLESPOON FINELY CHOPPED FRESH
    CILANTRO

1 SMALL CAN CRAB MEAT, THOROUGHLY
    DRAINED

1 POMELO OR PINK GRAPEFRUIT,
    SEGMENTED THEN HALVED

LETTUCE LEAVES, TO GARNISH

GRATED CARROT, TO GARNISH

METHOD

Place the ground meat in the water, and slowly cook over a medium heat until the meat turns color and is just cooked but still tender. Remove from the heat and let cool slightly. Add the lime juice, Nuoc Mam sauce, and chili to the meat. When thoroughly cooled, add the onion, ginger, cilantro, and crab meat, and stir thoroughly. Toss the grapefruit into the salad. Place the lettuce leaves on a flat dish. Arrange the grated carrot on the lettuce to form a ring. Spoon the salad into the center of the carrot.

serves 4

Balearic Garden Salad – SPAIN

This pretty, fresh salad includes fruit and the local capers, which grow on the Balearic hillsides and are sold pickled to the whole of Spain.

METHOD

Line a big plate or shallow salad bowl with the tomato slices. Beat together the oil, vinegar, salt, and black pepper in a bowl, and put the pear and apple slices into this as they are ready, turning to coat them (otherwise they will discolor). Arrange these over the tomatoes. Arrange the bell pepper rings on top, and sprinkle with the white and green of the scallions. Tuck bunches of purslane or watercress around the plate and in between the tomato. Dot with pieces of crumbled crackers and capers, and sprinkle with the remaining vinaigrette.

INGREDIENTS

3 FIRM TOMATOES, SLICED IN RINGS
¼ CUP OLIVE OIL
3 TABLESPOONS VINEGAR
PINCH OF SALT
FRESHLY GROUND BLACK PEPPER
1 RIPE PEAR, PEELED, CORED AND DICED
1 APPLE, CORED AND SLICED
2 GREEN BELL PEPPERS, SEEDED,
    AND SLICED IN RINGS
2 SCALLIONS, CHOPPED
SMALL BUNCH OF PURSLANE OR
    WATERCRESS TIPS
2 CRACKERS FOR CHEESE
½ CUP CAPERS

serves 4

Shrimp-Melon Salad – AMERICA

Lettuce from Kentucky, shrimp from the coastal waters and cantaloupe from Southern farms make a light and tasty summer salad, topped with a slightly sweet dressing.

METHOD

Toss the shrimp with the lime juice, and let them sit, refrigerated, about 30 minutes before preparing the salad. Divide the lettuce among four plates. Add shrimp, melon, and scallions. Pour the dressing over each salad and serve.

INGREDIENTS

1 PINT MEDIUM OR LARGE SHRIMP,
    COOKED AND CLEANED
2–3 TABLESPOONS LIME JUICE
ABOUT ½ MEDIUM LETTUCE, WASHED
    AND TORN INTO BITE-SIZE PIECES
1¾ CUPS CANTALOUPE BALLS
2 SCALLIONS, CHOPPED

FOR THE DRESSING

½ CUP OLIVE OR OTHER VEGETABLE OIL
4 TABLESPOONS LIME JUICE
1 TABLESPOON HONEY
2 TEASPOONS FINELY CHOPPED CHIVES
1 TEASPOON DIJON MUSTARD
SALT AND FRESHLY GROUND
    BLACK PEPPER

serves 4

Salad of Baby Squid with Oil, Garlic and Chili Peppers – ITALY

INGREDIENTS

2 PINTS BABY SQUID

JUICE OF 1 LEMON

1¼ CUPS OLIVE OIL

6 MEDIUM GARLIC CLOVES, SLICED NOT CRUSHED

3 FRESH GREEN CHILIES, SLICED AND SEEDED

SALT AND FRESHLY GROUND BLACK PEPPER

serves 4 to 6

METHOD

Clean the squid, and slice the bodies into rings. Bring at least four times the volume of water as you have squid to a brisk boil. Add the lemon juice. Plunge the prepared squid into the boiling water, and cook until the flesh loses its translucency. This will take no longer than 1 minute. Immediately remove the squid from the pan, and plunge it into cold water to stop the cooking process. In a separate saucepan, heat the olive oil until one piece of garlic sizzles fiercely when dropped in. Add all the garlic. Cook at a high heat for 30 seconds or so, then remove from the heat. The garlic will continue to cook. When the garlic pieces have turned mid-brown, add the sliced chili and return the pan to the heat for 30 seconds longer. Remove the pan from the heat, and let the cooking continue. Both garlic and chili should now be dark brown and crunchy. Let the oil, garlic, and chili cool before you dress the seasoned squid with it.

Bread Salad – LEBANON

INGREDIENTS

2 LARGE POCKET BREADS, TOASTED

JUICE OF 1½ LEMONS

1 CUCUMBER, SEEDED AND CUBED

6 SCALLIONS, CHOPPED

1 SMALL GREEN BELL PEPPER, CORED, SEEDED AND FINELY CHOPPED

4 PLUM TOMATOES, SEEDED, DRAINED AND CHOPPED

2 GARLIC CLOVES, CRUSHED

1 TABLESPOON FLAT-LEAFED PARSLEY, FINELY CHOPPED

1 TABLESPOON FINELY CHOPPED FRESH CILANTRO

½ CUP OLIVE OIL

SALT AND FRESHLY GROUND BLACK PEPPER

serves 6

METHOD

Cut the toasted bread into small pieces, and place in a bowl. Squeeze over the juice from ½ lemon and toss. Set aside for 5 minutes. In a larger bowl combine all the other ingredients, with salt and pepper to taste. Toss gently, add the bread and additional lemon juice, and combine. Serve the salad immediately.

Kentucky Fried Chicken Salad – AMERICA

Make salad into a main dish with the addition of warm strips of fried chicken. For ease of cooking and slicing, use boneless chicken breasts. Top with a favorite buttermilk-style dressing.

METHOD

Mix the flour and seasonings. Dredge the chicken breasts in seasoned flour. Heat ¼ inch oil in a skillet. When it's hot but not smoking, carefully add the chicken. Fry over medium heat, turning once, until outside is crispy and no pink is visible when you cut into the chicken, 10 to 15 minutes, depending on the thickness of the chicken. Let the chicken cool slightly. While it is cooling, divide the lettuce, mushrooms, celery, scallions and olives between two plates. Cut the chicken into strips, and arrange on top of the salad. Serve with buttermilk-style dressing.

INGREDIENTS FOR THE CHICKEN

3½ CUPS ALL-PURPOSE FLOUR

¼ TEASPOON SALT

½ TEASPOON PAPRIKA

¼ TEASPOON FRESHLY GROUND BLACK PEPPER

¼ TEASPOON DRIED THYME

⅛ TEASPOON CELERY SALT

2 CHICKEN BREASTS, BONELESS

OIL FOR FRYING

serves 2

Spaghetti and Salami Salad – ITALY

METHOD

Cut the spaghetti into 2-inch lengths, then cook it in boiling salted water for 3 minutes. Drain the pasta well in a fine strainer before tipping it into a bowl; let cool. Roast the pine kernels in a small, dry heavy-bottomed saucepan until they are lightly browned, then tip them over the pasta. Add the salami, olives, and artichoke hearts.

Mix the cider vinegar, seasoning, and sugar in a screw-top jar. Shake well until the sugar dissolves, then add the olive oil and shake again. Pour the dressing over the salad, and mix well. Toss the parsley in after the dressing, immediately before serving the salad.

INGREDIENTS

12 OUNCES FRESH SPAGHETTI

4 TABLESPOONS PINE KERNELS

6 OUNCES SALAMI, CUT IN STRIPS

⅓ CUP PITTED AND SLICED BLACK OLIVES

15-OUNCE CAN ARTICHOKE HEARTS, DRAINED

2 TABLESPOONS CIDER VINEGAR

SALT AND FRESHLY GROUND BLACK PEPPER

½ TEASPOON SUGAR

6 TABLESPOONS OLIVE OIL

4 TABLESPOONS CHOPPED PARSLEY

serves 4

Cold Jambalaya Salad Louisiana-style – AMERICA

This salad is a great make-ahead dish, and a great way to use up leftovers. For an elegant dish, mound the salad on a serving platter or a pretty ceramic pie dish, then circle it with wedges of tomatoes and/or lemons, and top it with several large cooked shrimp and a sprig of parsley.

INGREDIENTS

1 TABLESPOON BUTTER

1 ONION, CHOPPED

1 GARLIC CLOVE, FINELY CHOPPED

3 TABLESPOONS DICED COOKED HAM

1 TEASPOON SALT

¼ TEASPOON CAYENNE PEPPER

1 BAY LEAF

1⅓ CUPS WHITE RICE

2 TABLESPOONS GOOD-QUALITY OLIVE
   OIL

1 TABLESPOON WINE OR BALSAMIC
   VINEGAR

1 TABLESPOON LEMON JUICE

FEW DROPS OF TABASCO SAUCE, IF
   DESIRED

3 SCALLIONS, CHOPPED

2 CELERY STALKS, CHOPPED

1 SMALL GREEN BELL PEPPER, CHOPPED

2 MEDIUM TOMATOES, SEEDED AND CUT
   INTO BITE-SIZE CHUNKS

3 CUPS ANY COMBINATION OF COOKED
   SHRIMP, CRAB OR CHICKEN

serves 6

METHOD

In a medium saucepan, melt the butter. Sauté the onion and garlic until wilted, about 5 minutes. Add 2 cups water, the ham, and seasonings, and bring to a boil. Stir in the rice and return to the boil. Reduce the heat to very low, cover and cook until liquid is absorbed and the top of the rice is pitted with steam holes, 15 to 20 minutes. Fluff the rice with a fork. Cover, remove from the heat, and let sit for 5 to 10 minutes. Chill or let sit until cold. Remove the bay leaf. In a large bowl, toss the rice with the olive oil, vinegar, and lemon juice. Taste and adjust flavourings, and add Tabasco sauce if desired. Stir in the remaining ingredients, garnish and serve.

Ham and Avocado Salad – ITALY

INGREDIENTS

12 OUNCES FRESH PASTA SHAPES

2 TABLESPOONS CIDER VINEGAR

1 TEASPOON PREPARED WHOLEGRAIN
   MUSTARD

½ TEASPOON SUGAR

SALT AND FRESHLY GROUND
   BLACK PEPPER

6 TABLESPOONS OLIVE OIL

1 POUND LEAN COOKED HAM (IN ONE
   PIECE), CUBED

2 AVOCADOS

4 TABLESPOONS SNIPPED CHIVES

½ CUP CHOPPED WALNUTS

1 LETTUCE HEART OR ½ ICEBERG
   LETTUCE, SHREDDED (OPTIONAL)

serves 4

METHOD

Cook the pasta in boiling salted water for 3 minutes, then drain well. Meanwhile, mix the cider vinegar, mustard, sugar, and seasoning in a bowl. Whisk the mixture until the sugar and salt have dissolved. Gradually whisk in the oil. Turn the hot pasta into a dish, and pour the dressing over it; then mix well. Let the pasta cool slightly before mixing in the ham.

Just before serving the salad, halve the avocados, remove their pits and quarter the halves lengthways. Remove the peel, then cut the flesh into chunks, and mix them with the pasta. Mix in the chives and walnuts. Arrange the salad on a base of shredded lettuce, if liked, and serve promptly. If the salad is left to stand, the avocado will discolor.

Ham and avocado salad ▶

Warm Pasta Salad – AMERICA

This salad combines the saltiness of green olives, the crunch of walnuts, and the goodness of fresh vegetables. Use freshly grated Parmesan cheese, not the packaged kind; you'll notice a big difference in flavor. The flavors are enhanced when this salad is served warm, but if you have any cold leftovers, add a splash of vinaigrette for flavor.

INGREDIENTS

8 OUNCES FUSILLI OR OTHER PASTA

6 STALKS ASPARAGUS

3 TABLESPOONS EXTRA-VIRGIN OLIVE OIL

⅓ CUP FRESHLY GRATED PARMESAN
    CHEESE, PLUS EXTRA FOR TOPPING

½ SMALL ZUCCHINI, THINLY SLICED

2 SCALLIONS, CHOPPED

½ CUP WALNUT PIECES

½ CUP QUARTERED GREEN OLIVES

SALT AND FRESHLY GROUND
    BLACK PEPPER

serves 4

METHOD

Cook pasta according to directions on package. While the pasta is cooking, blanch the asparagus for 2 to 3 minutes in boiling water. Drain asparagus, then cut into 1-inch pieces. When the pasta is cooked, drain but do not rinse; then put it in a large mixing bowl. Pour olive oil over pasta, and toss with two forks. Add the Parmesan and toss again. Stir in the asparagus, zucchini, scallions, walnuts, and green olives. Add salt and pepper to taste. Serve with a sprinkling of Parmesan over the top.

Tagliatelle Nests – ITALY

These make a good first course or a light lunch.

INGREDIENTS

12 OUNCES FRESH TAGLIATELLE VERDI

2 TOMATOES, PEELED, SEEDED AND
    DICED

2 TABLESPOONS WALNUT OIL

3 TABLESPOONS SUNFLOWER OIL

JUICE OF 1 LIME

SALT AND FRESHLY GROUND
    BLACK PEPPER

1 TABLESPOON CHOPPED MINT

10 SLICES RINDLESS BACON

¾ CUP FROZEN PEAS

4 SMALL ZUCCHINI

4 TABLESPOONS SOUR CREAM

MINT SPRIGS, TO GARNISH (OPTIONAL)

serves 4

METHOD

Cook the tagliatelle in boiling salted water for 3 minutes, then drain well and put into a bowl. Add the tomatoes, both types of oil, the lime juice, some seasoning, and the mint. Toss well, cover and let cool. Grill the bacon slices until they are crisp, turning once. Drain them on paper towels and let cool. Cook the peas in boiling water for 15 minutes, then drain and set aside. Trim the zucchini, peel them very thinly so that they are a bright green outside, then halve them lengthways. Slice the zucchini thinly, and mix them with the peas. Divide the tagliatelle and its dressing between four plates, swirling it into nests. Top the nests with the zucchini and pea mixture. Crush the crisply broiled bacon, and sprinkle it over the zucchini and pea mixture; then top with a little sour cream. Mint sprigs may be added as a garnish, if liked.

Florida-style Tropical Pork Salad with Orange-Mint Dressing – AMERICA

METHOD

Whisk together the orange rind and juice, vinegar, mint, mustard, salt and pepper in a large bowl. Gradually whisk in the oil until blended. Gently stir in the pork, papaya, avocado, and onion, tossing to mix and coat. Mound the salad on a serving dish lined with lettuce, spinach or endive, and sprinkle with almonds.

INGREDIENTS

1 FINELY GRATED ORANGE RIND

¼ CUP FRESH ORANGE JUICE

1½ TABLESPOONS CIDER VINEGAR

2 TABLESPOONS CHOPPED FRESH MINT LEAVES, OR 1 TABLESPOON DRIED

¾ TEASPOON FRENCH MUSTARD

¼ TEASPOON SALT

¼ TEASPOON BLACK PEPPER

½ CUP OLIVE OIL

3 CUPS SHREDDED COOKED PORK

1 LARGE RIPE PAPAYA (1 POUND) PEELED, HALVED, SEEDED AND CUT INTO ½-INCH CHUNKS

1 RIPE AVOCADO (10 OUNCES) HALVED, PITTED, PEELED AND CUT INTO ½-INCH CHUNKS

1 SMALL RED ONION, THINLY SLICED

5 OUNCES LETTUCE, FRESH SPINACH OR ENDIVE TORN INTO PIECES

⅓ CUP SLIVERED ALMONDS, TOASTED

serves 4

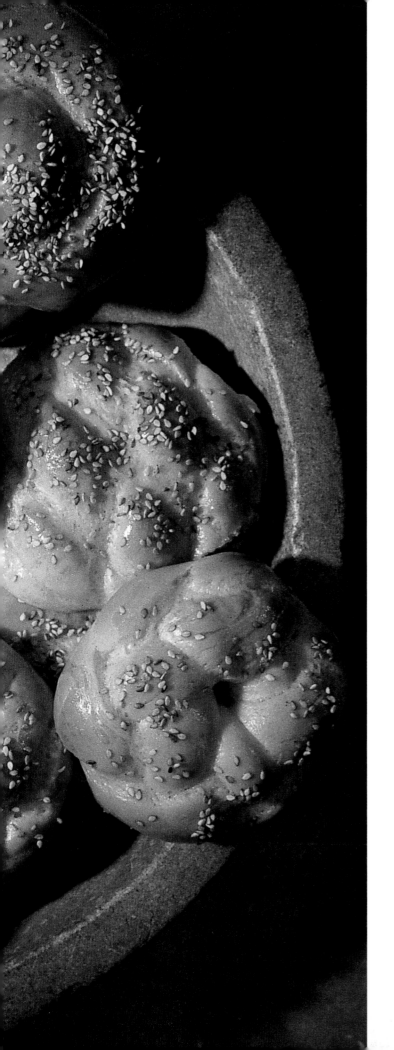

Breads

~

Sesame Rolls – GREECE

These make excellent rolls for all occasions, so freeze whatever you don't need immediately, and thaw a few at a time as you require them.

INGREDIENTS

2 TABLESPOONS DRY YEAST

14 CUPS ALL-PURPOSE FLOUR

1 CUP FINE GRANUALTED SUGAR

5 TABLESPOONS WARM WATER

2½ CUPS MILK

3 EGGS, BEATEN

FEW DROPS OF VANILLA EXTRACT

½ CUP MELTED UNSALTED BUTTER

VEGETABLE OIL, FOR GREASING

1 EGG, BEATEN, TO GLAZE

SESAME SEEDS, TO DECORATE

serves 24

METHOD

Place the yeast, 3 tablespoons flour, ½ teaspoon sugar, ½ teaspoon salt, and the warm water in a small bowl. Stir until the yeast and sugar have dissolved, then cover with plastic wrap, and leave in a warm place for about 15 minutes or until frothy. Place the milk in a large mixing bowl, and stir in the remaining sugar and salt, the beaten eggs, and the vanilla extract. Stir in the frothy yeast mixture, and beat well. Sift half of the remaining flour into the mixing bowl, and beat well. Add the melted butter and beat, adding the remaining flour, sifting it in as required to make a stiff dough. Transfer the dough onto a lightly floured surface, and knead for about 10 minutes or until the dough is smooth and elastic. Return to the cleaned bowl, cover with plastic wrap, and leave in a warm place for about 1½ hours or until doubled in size. Turn the dough out, and punch down to its original size. Return the dough to the bowl, cover, and leave in a warm place for another hour until risen. Turn the dough out onto a lightly floured surface, and punch down to its original size. Divide the dough into about forty eight pieces, the size of a walnut. Roll each piece into a 7-inch sausage shape, and twist, tie or coil it into an attractive design for a

bread roll. Place the shapes on greased baking sheets, and loosely cover with plastic wrap. Leave in a warm place for 30 minutes to rise. Preheat the oven to 350°F. Carefully brush each roll with the beaten egg to glaze, and sprinkle generously with sesame seeds. Bake for about 15 to 20 minutes, in batches if necessary, until the rolls are golden brown, risen and hollow-sounding when tapped underneath. Transfer to a wire rack to cool before serving.

Lithuanian Cottage Cheese Bacon Bread – RUSSIAN FEDERATION

***Varske* – cottage cheese – and honey are commonly used as a baking ingredient in Lithuania. This recipe mixes wholewheat and white flour to give a hint of the sturdier type of bread you will find in the Baltic States.**

INGREDIENTS

¼ CUP VEGETABLE OIL

1¼ CUPS FINELY CHOPPED LEAN BACON

2 HEAPED TABLESPOONS FINELY
   CHOPPED SCALLIONS

4 TABLESPOONS HONEY

¾ CUP MILK

1 EGG

¾ CUP COTTAGE CHEESE

1¼ CUPS WHOLEWHEAT FLOUR

1¼ CUPS WHITE BREAD FLOUR

2 TEASPOONS BAKING POWDER

½ TEASPOON BAKING SODA

1 TEASPOON SALT

makes 1 loaf

METHOD

In a small saucepan, heat the vegetable oil over medium-high heat. Add the bacon, and fry for a few minutes, until the bacon is cooked. Turn down the heat, and stir in the scallions, letting them wilt slightly. Then add the honey, heat through, and remove from the stove. Beat in the milk, egg, and then the cottage cheese. Blend thoroughly and set aside. In a large bowl, sift together the two flours, baking powder and soda, and salt. Make a well, and pour in the cottage cheese mixture, beating gently – do not overbeat. Preheat the oven to 375°F. Scrape the bread dough into a buttered and floured 9 x 5 x 3-inch loaf pan. Flatten the top of the loaf with a spatula, and drop the loaf sharply twice on a hard surface to eliminate air pockets. Bake for 45 to 50 minutes, or until the top is golden brown. Place the pan on a wire rack to cool for 15 minutes before inverting. Cool completely before serving.

Lithuanian cottage cheese bread ▶

Sesame Sticks – THAILAND

INGREDIENTS

½ CAKE COMPRESSED YEAST OR
   1 TEASPOON DRY YEAST
1 TEASPOON SUGAR
3 CUPS ALL-PURPOSE FLOUR
1 TEASPOON SALT
PINCH OF CAYENNE
1 TEASPOON GROUND CUMIN
1 EGG, LIGHTLY BEATEN
¼ CUP MELTED BUTTER
APPROX. ⅔ CUP WARM WATER
¼ CUP SESAME SEEDS

serves 6

METHOD

Preheat the oven to 350°F. Cream the yeast and sugar together. Sift the flour, salt and spices into a warmed bowl, and make a well. Stir in the yeast mixture, egg, melted butter and half the water. Gradually add enough of the remaining water to form a soft dough. Knead for about 10 minutes then put into a clean bowl, cover with a dish towel, and let stand in a warm place until doubled in size, which can take up to 2 hours. Roll golf-ball sized pieces of the dough into sausages about ⅓ inch wide, and cut into 4-inch lengths. Reroll any scraps. Roll the dough sticks in sesame seeds, and arrange them, 1 inch apart, on ungreased baking sheets. Bake in a preheated oven for 25 to 30 minutes, until golden brown and crisped through. Serve warm.

Variation For Honey Sesame Sticks, use only ½ teaspoon salt, substitute 2 teaspoons finely ground aniseed for the cayenne and cumin, and glaze with 3 tablespoons warmed honey halfway through baking.

Garlic Straws – FRANCE

INGREDIENTS

8 OUNCES PUFF PASTRY DOUGH
JUICE OF 2–3 GARLIC CLOVES
¼ CUP MILK
1 TEASPOON PAPRIKA
1 TABLESPOON GRATED PARMESAN
   CHEESE
SALT AND CAYENNE PEPPER

serves 6

METHOD

Preheat the oven to 425°F. Roll out the pastry dough on a floured board into a rectangle, as thinly as possible. Stir the garlic juice into most of the milk, and brush the dough with half of it. Mix the paprika and Parmesan, and season with a little salt and cayenne. Sprinkle half of it over one half of the dough. Fold the dough and roll out as thinly as possible. Repeat with the remaining garlic milk and Parmesan mixture, and roll out to a rectangle not more than ¼ inch thick. Brush with milk, and cut into strips about ½ inch wide and 6 inches long. Arrange the straws, at least 1 inch apart, on greased baking sheets, and bake for 7 to 10 minutes or until well-risen and golden brown. Serve warm, piled onto each other, log cabin-style.

Sesame Bread Rings – LEBANON

In Lebanon these sesame rings are made by bakeries; in some other countries they are more commonly sold on street corners. The *mahlab* imparts a typical flavor found only in Arab baked goods. Broken into pieces, this bread makes a good alternative to pocket bread or for dips.

METHOD

In a bowl combine ¼ cup lukewarm water with the yeast and sugar. Let it stand for about 3 minutes, then stir. Let rest in a warm place for about 6 minutes. Put the flour in a large, warmed bowl, and stir in the salt and ground *mahlab*. Make a well in the center and pour in the yeast and sugar mixture. Work the butter into the flour, and add 5 to 6½ tablespoons water to the dough, a spoonful at a time, until you have a firm dough that can be moved to a floured work surface. Preheat the oven to 300°F. Knead the dough, pressing, pushing and folding, for about 10 minutes, until it is smooth and elastic. Transfer to a bowl, cover with a cloth, and leave in a warm place for 15 minutes. Punch down the dough with a couple of punches, and divide it into twelve pieces. On a floured work surface, roll each piece into a long "sausage" about the thickness of a finger. Shape the sausage into a round – or, less authentically but more decoratively, into a criss-crossed pretzel shape. Place the rings on an oiled baking sheet, cover with a cloth, and let rise for about 15 minutes. Brush each ring with some beaten egg, and sprinkle with sesame seeds. Bake for about 30 to 35 minutes, until golden. Transfer the rings to a cake rack to cool for 10 minutes before serving. The rings freeze successfully.

INGREDIENTS

1 ENVELOPE DRY YEAST

1 TEASPOON FINE GRANULATED SUGAR

2 CUPS WHITE BREAD FLOUR

½ TEASPOON SALT

1 TEASPOON GROUND *MAHLAB*

1 TABLESPOON MELTED BUTTER

1 EGG, BEATEN

3 TABLESPOONS SESAME SEEDS

serves 6 to 12

Dal Bread – INDIA

METHOD

Pick over the dal, wash well and cook in about 2½ cups of water for 10 to 15 minutes, until the dal can be mashed with the back of a wooden spoon. Drain well. Grind, pound or blend the dal, garlic, and green chili in a blender or food processor. Mix the cumin and turmeric with 1 teaspoon of water, and blend into the purée, which should be dry rather than loose. Sift the flour into a bowl, make a well in the middle, and add the butter or ghee, oil, baking powder, and ½ teaspoon of salt. Combine the ingredients to make a dough, adding as little warm water as possible, about 3 tablespoons. The dough should be soft but not sticky. Pull off a small piece of dough, and roll it into a ball on a lightly floured surface. Make a hollow in the ball and stuff in a spoonful of dal. Stretch the dough to cover the stuffing, then roll and flatten the ball to make a small pancake. Repeat with the remaining dough. Heat a flat pan without any fat or oil. Cook a pancake in the hot pan for about 2 minutes on each side, until speckled and puffy.

INGREDIENTS

1 CUP CHANNA DAL (SPLIT YELLOW PEAS)

4–6 GARLIC CLOVES, FINELY CHOPPED

2 FRESH GREEN CHILIES, FINELY CHOPPED

1 TEASPOON GROUND CUMIN

½ TEASPOON TURMERIC

3 CUPS ALL-PURPOSE FLOUR

¼ CUP DICED BUTTER OR GHEE

2 TABLESPOONS OIL

½ TEASPOON BAKING POWDER

½ TEASPOON SALT

serves 6 to 8

Nan Bread – INDIA

INGREDIENTS

1 CAKE COMPRESSED YEAST OR 1
    TABLESPOON DRY YEAST

1 TEASPOON SUGAR

1 CUP ALL-PURPOSE FLOUR, WARMED

1½ TEASPOONS SALT

1½ TEASPOONS BAKING POWDER

2 TABLESPOONS OIL

6 TABLESPOONS NATURAL YOGURT

1 CUP WARM WATER

PINCH OF GARAM MASALA

serves 10

METHOD

Preheat the oven to 475°F. Cream the yeast and sugar together. Sift the flour, salt and baking powder into a bowl, and make a well. Pour the yeast, oil, yogurt, and most of the water, and mix well. The mixture should be fairly soft. Knead the dough until it no longer sticks to your fingers, about 10 minutes. Put the dough into an oiled polythene bag, and leave in a warm place until doubled in size. This could take 1½ to 3 hours, depending on the temperature. Punch down the dough, and divide it into 10 pieces.

Either roll out on a floured surface or toss from hand to hand – flour them well first – to form an oblong about ¼ inch thick. Sprinkle with garam masala, and bake for about 10 minutes, turning once, until puffed and beginning to brown. Serve warm.

Variation Halfway through baking, the Nan can be glazed with beaten egg yolk and sprinkled with poppy seeds.

Garlic Bread – FRANCE

METHOD
Preheat the oven to 450°F. Crush the peeled garlic cloves with salt. Blend the crushed garlic into the butter. Add the chopped parsley and seasoning. Place the bread in the hot oven for 15 minutes. Slice the bread, smother with the butter and serve.

There are several savory alternatives to this recipe:

Add 2 teaspoons of tomato paste to the butter, smother slices of bread with the pink butter and toast.

Use ¾ cup butter and 1 cup grated cheese, instead of 1 cup butter. Mix together with the flavorings. Heat the bread, slice, smother with the cheesy butter, and return to the oven to melt the cheese.

INGREDIENTS
1 LARGE FRENCH STICK OR BAGUETTE

1 CUP BUTTER, SOFTENED TO ROOM TEMPERATURE

2 TEASPOONS GARLIC, PEELED BY PLACING ON A BAKING SHEET IN A HOT OVEN FOR 10 MINUTES (THE GARLIC WILL POP OUT OF ITS SKIN)

1 TABLESPOON CHOPPED FRESH PARSLEY

SALT AND FRESHLY GROUND BLACK PEPPER

serves 4

Arab Bread – LEBANON

Versions of this bread are found all over the Arab world, made at village bakeries and in backyard ovens of packed earth. The recipe is a simple one, but the bread itself is heavenly – a light, puffy round with a slightly gritty quality. It must be eaten immediately, however, as it becomes hard and crumbly as it stands, unless it is quickly covered.

INGREDIENTS

2 PACKETS DRY YEAST

8 CUPS CHAPATI FLOUR OR WHITE
BREAD FLOUR

½ TEASPOON SALT

¼ CUP OLIVE OIL

CHAPATI FLOUR OR CORNMEAL, FOR
DUSTING

serves 8

METHOD

Combine ¼ cup lukewarm water with the yeast in a bowl. Let it stand for about 3 minutes, then stir to make sure that all of the yeast is dissolved. Let rest in a warm place for 6 minutes, or until it has doubled in size. Put the flour in a large, warmed bowl, and stir in the salt. Make a well in the center and pour in the yeast mixture. Add the oil and 2 cups lukewarm water, working the latter in a few tablespoons at a time. Add a little more, if necessary, to make a firm dough that can be picked up and transferred to a floured work surface. Knead the dough, pressing, pushing and folding it, for about 20 minutes, or until it is smooth and elastic. Transfer the dough to the bowl, cover with a cloth, and leave in a warm place for 2 hours, until doubled in bulk and bubbly. Place the dough on the work surface and punch down with a couple of knuckle punches. Divide the dough into eight pieces, and shape them into balls. Scatter the chapati flour or cornmeal on the work surface, and roll out four of the balls into 8-inch rounds. As you roll out each round, place it on a baking sheet covered with a cloth. Repeat with the remaining balls on another baking sheet. Leave both covered sheets of bread to rise for another 30 minutes. Preheat the oven to 400°F. Place both sheets, one above the other, as low in the oven as possible. Bake at this level for 5 minutes, then move them to the center of the oven, placing the sheet that was lower on top. Continue baking for 4 to 5 minutes longer, or until the rounds are puffed and golden. Remove from the oven and serve immediately. The rounds can be kept covered in foil in a low oven or warm place, if not needed immediately.

Unleavened Bread – INDIA

METHOD

Sift the flour into a bowl with the salt, and combine with as little boiling water as possible, about 3 tablespoons, to make a dough that is soft but not sticky. Form the dough into balls, roll and flatten them on a lightly floured surface to make small pancakes. Heat a pan without fat or oil, and cook for about 2 minutes on each side, until speckled and puffy.

INGREDIENTS

2 CUPS ALL-PURPOSE FLOUR

½ TEASPOON SALT

BOILING WATER

serves 4 to 6

Pan Bagna – ITALY

METHOD

Slice off the top third of the loaf, and scoop out most of the inside (this can be used as bread crumbs in other recipes). Heat the oil, and fry the onion and garlic until the onion begins to brown; then turn down the heat, and cook until the onions are transparent. Add the tomatoes, olives, oregano, and sugar, and season with salt and plenty of freshly ground black pepper. Stir well and take off the heat. Fill the scooped-out loaf with this mixture, and replace the top. Wrap the filled loaf in foil, and enclose in a plastic bag. Weight it down with a plate and several cans. Leave in the refrigerator for 2 to 4 hours. Serve cold in thick slices. This is superb picnic food.

Variation Omit the onion and use 1½ pounds tomatoes. Mix together the tomatoes, garlic, oil, olives, and sugar, and season well. Replace the dried oregano with 2 teaspoons of finely chopped fresh basil or marjoram.

INGREDIENTS

1 MEDIUM-SIZED WHITE LOAF

2 TABLESPOONS OLIVE OIL

1 LARGE ONION, THINLY SLICED

2–3 GARLIC CLOVES, FINELY CHOPPED

12 OUNCES TOMATOES, PEELED, SEEDED AND SLICED

12 PITTED BLACK OLIVES

½ TEASPOON DRIED OREGANO

½ TEASPOON SUGAR

SALT AND FRESHLY GROUND BLACK PEPPER

serves 4

Classic Olive Bread — GREECE

INGREDIENTS

7 CUPS BREAD FLOUR

1 TABLESPOON BAKING POWDER

PINCH OF SALT

¼ CUP WATER

¼ CUP OLIVE OIL PLUS EXTRA FOR
   GREASING

1 TABLESPOON DRIED MINT

1 ONION, FINELY CHOPPED

GENEROUS 2 CUPS PITTED, RINSED AND
   DRIED OLIVES

1 EGG YOLK, BEATEN, TO GLAZE

serves 6

The olives in this bread are sometimes added unpitted. For an extra-luxurious finish, brush the bread with some beaten egg yolk 15 minutes before the end of the cooking time.

METHOD

Preheat the oven to 375°F. Sift the flour, baking powder and salt together in a large mixing bowl, and make a well in the center. Pour the water into the well with the olive oil, dried mint, chopped onion and the olives. Stir well with a wooden spoon to form a stiff dough. Transfer the mixture to a lightly floured work surface, and knead the dough for at least 10 minutes until smooth and soft. Return to the cleaned bowl, cover with plastic wrap, and let rest for about 10 minutes. Transfer the dough once more to a lightly floured work surface. Knead and shape into 9½-inch round. Lightly oil a 10-inch pie dish, and place the dough in it. Bake for about 50 minutes, brushing the surface of the bread with the beaten egg yolk 15 minutes before the end of the cooking time. Transfer the bread to a wire rack to cool before serving.

Sesame Pitta Bread — MIDDLE EAST

METHOD

In a blender or food processor, blend the flour and salt for 2 to 3 seconds to combine. In a measuring jug or medium bowl, combine the yeast, sugar, and ½ cup lukewarm water, stirring, until yeast is almost dissolved, 1 to 2 minutes. Let stand until surface looks bubbly and foaming, 10 to 12 minutes. Stir 1 cup lukewarm water into the yeast mixture. With machine running, gradually pour in the yeast liquid. If dough looks too dry, add a little water, 1 tablespoon at a time, and blend until a ball of dough forms. Blend for 1 minute. Lightly oil a bowl, place the dough in the bowl, and turn to coat with oil. (This prevents a crust from forming on the surface.) Cover the dough with a damp dish towel, and let rise in a warm place until doubled in bulk, 1½ to 2 hours. Transfer the dough to a lightly floured surface, and knead lightly. Roll the dough into a long, thick log, and cut into about 12 equal-size pieces. Roll each piece into a smooth ball, flouring the surface only if necessary. Place balls on a floured baking sheet, and cover with the dish towel. Let rise until doubled in bulk, about 30 minutes. In a small bowl, pour about ½ inch sesame seeds. Roll each ball into the sesame seeds to coat well; add more seeds to the bowl as needed. On a lightly floured surface, roll each ball into a 5 to 6-inch round. Preheat the oven to 450°F or highest setting. Lightly flour 2 large baking sheets. Place 3 to 4 dough rounds on each sheet, and bake until just beginning to brown, about 3 minutes. Turn over and bake until lightly browned, 2 to 3 minutes. Repeat with the remaining dough. Serve.

INGREDIENTS

4 CUPS BREAD FLOUR

1 TEASPOON SALT

1 TABLESPOON DRY YEAST

1 TEASPOON SUGAR

1½ CUPS LUKEWARM WATER

SESAME SEEDS, FOR ROLLING

serves 12

Oven-Crisped Bread with Tomato and Fresh Basil — ITALY

METHOD

In a low oven, toast the bread until each slice is completely dry and crisp. Coarsely dice the tomatoes (there is no need to peel them), and finely chop the basil. Add the basil, olive oil, and seasoning to the tomatoes. Spoon on top of the bread slices, and serve immediately. (The bread should still be slightly warm.)

INGREDIENTS

6 SLICES THICKLY CUT WHITE BREAD, PREFERABLY ITALIAN

1 POUND FRESH TOMATOES

1 CUP FRESH BASIL

¼ CUP OLIVE OIL

SALT AND FRESHLY GROUND BLACK PEPPER

serves 6

Pocket Bread – GREECE

INGREDIENTS

6 TEASPOON DRY YEAST

1 TEASPOON FINE GRANULATED SUGAR

2½ CUPS WARM WATER

12 CUPS BREAD FLOUR, PLUS EXTRA FOR
    DREDGING

2 TEASPOONS SALT

⅓ CUP MELTED BUTTER

serves 12

There's nothing quite like the taste of freshly baked pocket bread, served with an array of tempting dishes at the *Meze* table. Pitta bread freezes well, too. You can thaw it out and warm it up by putting it in a medium oven for just a few minutes before serving.

METHOD

Place the yeast and sugar in a small bowl, and add 1¼ cups warm water. Stir to dissolve the yeast and sugar. Cover with plastic wrap, and stand in a warm place for about 15 minutes or until frothy. Place the flour and salt in a large mixing bowl, and make a well in the center. Pour 1¼ cups warm water into the well, and add the melted butter and the yeast mixture. Stir to form a sticky dough. Transfer the dough to a lightly floured surface, adding a little extra flour to the dough if necessary, and knead until smooth and soft. Shape the dough into a ball, and place in the cleaned mixing bowl. Cover with plastic wrap and stand in a warm place for about 1½ hours, or until the dough has doubled in size. Transfer the dough to a lightly floured surface, and punch down to its original size. Let the dough rest for about 20 minutes. Meanwhile, dredge three baking sheets with flour. Cut the dough into 12 equal portions and roll each one into an 8-inch round. Place the rounds on the baking sheets, leaving about 1 inch between them. Cover loosely with plastic wrap, and return to a warm place to prove again for about 30 minutes. Preheat the oven to 475°F. Place one of the baking sheets on the bottom of the oven for 3 to 5 minutes, or until the breads have puffed up. Remove the breads from the baking sheet, and place them on the middle oven rack; bake for about 5 minutes, or until firm and just beginning to brown. Place on a warm serving platter, and repeat with the remaining pocket breads. Serve warm.

Polish Rye Bread – POLAND

METHOD

Combine the flours and salt in a large bowl, and set aside. Combine the yeast, sugar and caraway seeds in the bowl of an electric mixer fitted with the dough hook. Add oil and 1 cup lukewarm water, and stir, sprinkle with a little flour. Cover bowl with a clean dish towel, and leave until mixture looks slightly foamy and bubbly, 10 to 12 minutes. With the mixer on low speed, pour in 1½ cups lukewarm water, and beat until combined. Gradually add the flours; when completely incorporated, the dough will be sticky. You may have some flour mixture left over. Increase the mixer to medium speed, and knead dough until dough forms a soft ball around the dough hook and leaves side of bowl, 5 to 7 minutes. If the dough remains very sticky, add a little more flour, and continue to knead for 2 minutes. (Do not add too much more flour or the bread will be tough.) Lightly grease a bowl, and place the dough in it; turn the dough to coat with oil. (This prevents a crust from forming on surface.) Cover bowl with a dish towel, and let rise until doubled in bulk, 1½ to 2 hours, in a warm, draft-free place. Lightly grease a large baking sheet. Transfer the dough to a lightly floured surface, and knead gently to knock the air out of it. Cut the dough in half, and shape each half into a smooth round ball. Place each loaf on opposite corners of the baking sheet, flatten slightly and cover with a towel. Let the loaves rise again until almost doubled in size, 1 hour. Preheat oven to 350°F. Brush the loaves with egg glaze or melted butter or margarine. With a sharp knife, slash the top of each loaf 2 or 3 times. Bake until the loaves are well browned and sound hollow when tapped on the bottom, 35 to 40 minutes. Remove to a wire rack to cool.

INGREDIENTS

8 CUPS ALL-PURPOSE FLOUR

3 CUPS RYE FLOUR

2 TEASPOONS SALT

2 TABLESPOONS ACTIVE DRY YEAST

1 TEASPOON SUGAR

2 TEASPOONS CARAWAY SEEDS

¾ CUP VEGETABLE OIL

2½ CUPS LUKEWARM WATER

1 EGG, BEATEN, OR 2 TABLESPOONS BUTTER OR MARGARINE, MELTED, FOR GLAZE

makes 2 loaves

Flour Tortillas – MEXICO

Light and flaky, these dough pancakes from the north of Mexico are far more delicate in flavor than the staple corn tortilla, and considerably easier to make. A very light touch is needed with the rolling pin; Mexican cooks use a short piece of broom handle as they find the conventional rolling pin too heavy. Serve them warm, wrapped around or spread with your choice of topping, or have them for breakfast with butter and jam.

METHOD

First of all cut 2 rounds 6 inches across, out of thin plastic – a polythene bag is ideal. Sift the flour and salt into a bowl and rub in the shortening. Add just enough water for the dough to hold together, then knead until it no longer feels sticky. Divide into 24 pieces, and roll each into a ball. Put a skillet or a griddle onto heat. No fat is necessary. Put a dough ball in the center of one of your plastic rounds. Flatten slightly and put the other round on top. Using these as a guide – and to stop the dough sticking to the work surface and the rolling pin – roll out your tortilla to a roughly circular shape, rotating the rolling pin at each stroke to get an even thickness. Remove the plastic before cooking the tortillas. Fry each tortilla for about 30 seconds on each side. They should puff slightly and have dark patches. As they are cooked, wrap them in a dish towel to keep them warm and supple. Cooked, they will keep for several days in the refrigerator, wrapped in their towel and a polythene bag, and they also freeze well. To reheat, dry fry for a few moments on each side.

INGREDIENTS

4 CUPS ALL-PURPOSE FLOUR

1½ TEASPOONS SALT

½ CUP WHITE VEGETABLE SHORTENING

1 CUP WATER

serves 6 to 12

Brown Soda-Bread – IRELAND

INGREDIENTS

8 CUPS WHOLEWHEAT FLOUR

4 CUPS WHITE BREAD FLOUR

1 HEAPED TEASPOON BAKING SODA

1 HEAPED TEASPOON BAKING POWDER

2½ CUPS NATURAL YOGHURT MIXED
  WITH WATER TO THE CONSISTENCY OF
  BUTTERMILK

2 EGGS

GOOD PINCH OF SALT

makes 2 loaves

METHOD

Preheat the oven to 375°F. Place all the dry ingredients in a large mixing bowl. Combine well with the fingers. In another bowl mix the eggs with the yogurt and water. Make a well in the dry mixture, and slowly pour on the yogurt and water. Mix with your hands until you get a nice soft dough – not too wet. A dough that is too wet or too stiff will result in a hard and heavy bread. Lightly flour a work surface. Divide the dough in half. Make two flat rounds of bread on the board. Cut a deep cross in the middle of each loaf. Bake for 10 minutes, then reduce the heat. Bake until the bottom of the bread sounds hollow when knocked. This takes about 30 minutes.

Bagels – ISRAEL

INGREDIENTS

1 TABLESPOON DRY YEAST

2 TABLESPOONS SUGAR

¼ CUP VEGETABLE OIL OR
  ¼ CUP MARGARINE

1 TEASPOON SALT

4 CUPS BREAD FLOUR

1 EGG, LIGHTLY BEATEN (OPTIONAL)

1 EGG, WELL BEATEN, FOR GLAZE

POPPY OR SESAME SEEDS (OPTIONAL)

makes 12

METHOD

Combine the yeast and 1 tablespoon sugar in a small bowl. Heat the remaining sugar, vegetable oil or margarine, and salt with 1 cup water, in a small saucepan over medium heat, stirring until blended. Pour into the yeast-sugar mixture, and stir until dissolved, 1 to 2 minutes. Let stand until surface becomes bubbly, 5 to 7 minutes. Place the flour in a blender or food processor. With the machine running, slowly pour the liquid into the flour until the mixture forms a ball of dough. If using an egg, add egg with liquid. Continue to process for 1 minute longer. Dough should be smooth and not sticky. Add a little more flour if the dough is too soft, and process for 30 seconds longer. Lightly oil a bowl, and place the dough in bowl; turn to coat the dough. (This prevents a crust from forming on the surface.) Cover the bowl with a clean dish towel, and leave in a warm place to rise until doubled in bulk, 1½ to 2 hours. Transfer the dough to lightly floured surface, and knead for 2 to 3 minutes. Divide dough into 12 equal-size pieces. Roll each piece into a log about 5½ inches long; wet one end slightly and shape into a ring, pressing the ends together firmly. Arrange the rings on a large, lightly floured baking sheet. Cover with a dish towel and let rise until almost doubled in size, 20 to 30 minutes. Preheat the oven to 400°F. Bring a large saucepan filled with water over high heat, to a gentle boil. Carefully slide 3 or 4 bagels into the water, and cook for 1 minute. Remove to paper towels to drain. Continue cooking bagels. Lightly grease 2 large baking sheets. Arrange 6 boiled bagels on each sheet. Brush with a little egg glaze. Sprinkle with poppy or sesame seeds, if using. Bake the bagels until well browned and crisp, 20 minutes. Transfer to wire rack to cool. Serve warm or cool completely, then reheat to serve if you like.

Bagels ▶